Civil Conversation

Book III

The manner of conversation to be observed all within the home.

By
Stefano Guazzo, 1574

Translated by
George Pettie, 1581

Adapted by
David Neitz, 2023

Edited by
Helen Bowden and Steven Neitz, 2023

Independently published

Copyright © 2023 David Neitz

All rights reserved.

ISBN: 9798399137100

Dedication

To my daughters Kristen and Kaitlyn, may the paths you travel bring you closer to your dreams.

Introduction

William and Anniball resume their discussion on the third day of civil conversation. The two acknowledge their growing friendship and look forward to the day's discussion as the conversation continues to flow back and forth.

This book focuses on conversation and behavior within the home and family. It provides insight into building a positive and supportive environment that encourages open communication and positive relationships. A sense of equality between parties should be the goal, but also an understanding of the roles each plays in helping to create a healthy and successful relationship. The times have changed since this was written in the late 16th century. Back then, people relied heavily on religion, superstition, and manual labor.

William and Anniball have a lengthy discussion on marriage. Though it is revealed early that they are both single, remember that Anniball is a doctor and makes house calls, it is the 16th century, and they were very religious.

At a glance, this book appears male-centric. Anniball presents a disclaimer at the beginning that father and son are synonymous with mother and daughter. Sisters are included with brothers, etc. The master and servant relationship is similar to that of an employer and employee. In both cases, one party is in charge, and the other is expected to follow instructions and work hard. The master is responsible for providing the servant with food, shelter, and protection, while the servant is expected to obey the master and do whatever tasks the master assigns. The modern employer-employee relationship is similar in that the employer provides a salary and other benefits. At the same time, the employee is responsible for doing their job and following the employer's instructions. Both relationships should be based on mutual trust and respect, and both involve an exchange of goods and services.

I hope you, the reader, enjoy this conversation as much as I did. You will have to read between the lines sometimes as you explore the nuances of the discussion and era.

Table of Contents

A friendship takes root	1
Marriage	5
Parents and children	65
Responsibilities of the father	104
Behavior of the child	108
A little bit about daughters	112
Differences between sons and daughters	121
Brothers	128
Masters and servants	142
A prescription for health	170
Bibliography	174
Index	176
Notes	179

A friendship takes root

*A conversation between
William Guazzo
and
Master Anniball Magnocavalli*

*A*nniball. No sooner had I set foot outside your door yesterday, I received a letter from a dear friend informing me that he was getting married in Genoa. He requested that I attend his wedding and visit such a wonderful city. I can visit Genoa and the gentlemen whenever I please, but I cannot enjoy our company at my leisure. I thanked him for the invitation, excusing myself as best I could. My return today is to do you a service and for my pleasure, because of your charming presence, the loss of which, all Genoa could not repay me.

William. With these words of yours, I feel

sorrow in two respects and pleasure in one. Love for my neighbor makes me share in your passion. I understand that for my sake you have deprived yourself of the pleasure which was prepared for you at the marriage of your special friend and the sight of such a famous city. I feel sorry for your friend because his hope of having your good company will be missed. My selfishness is so strong, my sorrows soon give way to the wonderful pleasure I take in seeing that you have more regard for me than him. If he should ever come to know this partiality on your part, I doubt if the goodwill he now bears you will not be somewhat diminished and he will resent me. For my part I will forgive him, hoping that he will eventually realize that it was okay to be bold with an old friend to satisfy a new one. I highly commend your wit and thank you most sincerely for it. Your desire to enrich my poor understanding with the treasure of your gentle and learned discourses is much appreciated. I pray that you continue to have a good opinion of me and I am worthy of that praise regarding me more highly than all the magnificence of Genoa.

Anniball. While it is true that my discourse enhances your virtue, it is also true that your witty inquiries improve my speech. Now, to return to our matter, we must explore (according to our decision yesterday) domestic conversation, that is, within the home, which we

A friendship takes root

shall also reduce to these two particular points, speech and behavior. I must tell you that I do not intend, in today's discussion, to establish how a man ought to govern a house well, nor how a master of the home ought to provide for the things about food, clothing, profits, expenses, buildings, cultivation of the land, and the preservation of their property. I intend to speak of the particular points that members of the same household should observe in conversation. To come to the point, most domestic conversations take place either between the husband and wife, father and son, brothers, or master and servant. Our discourse will consist of these four areas.

William. I think this division should have been larger. Seeing that in families there is the mother, daughter, uncle, nephew, father-in-law, son-in-law, stepmother, stepdaughter, cousins, and allies. I do not think that division is big enough.

Anniball. Under the name of father and son, I have included mother and daughter. The name brothers include sisters, master and man, and mistress and maid. I include uncle, father-in-law, and tutor under the name of father; son-in-law, daughter-in-law, and pupil under the name of son; cousins and allies under the name of brothers. In my opinion, the division made is not defective and requires no addition of superfluous things. Since the principal

Civil Conversation III

conversation comes through marriage, there can be no cities without families or families without a husband and wife. Let us start the discussion and begin with the conversation of the married, since the greatest honor is due to it, not only because it is the first in order, but also because there is no conversation more agreeable to nature, than that of the male and the female.

Marriage

William. Although our main purpose is to talk about the conversation between husband and wife, it wouldn't hurt if you first gave some good instructions to someone who intends to get married.

Anniball. I like your suggestion and it may be that this discussion has the power to awaken in our hearts the desire to get married.

William. I have heard it said that sometimes we have a desire or appetite which you physicians call excessive, to which you forbid meat. If the desire to marry a wife comes to me, I intend on my part to satisfy it only by abstinence. I remember the great praise that a philosopher gave to those who had a great desire to sail and yet never ventured out to sea; to govern the commonwealth, and yet never interfere with it;

Civil Conversation III

to marry a wife and yet married none. I think it is well to act on this point as did a man who, having been earnestly solicited by his mother to take a wife, replied that it was not yet the time. Some months later, being solicited by her on the same subject, replied that the time had passed.

Anniball. Some men are of such a delicate disposition, that they never know what they want and all human conditions are not easy for them. You know very well that the wise man, well resolved, settles down with a cheerful spirit to every hardship in life, and in particular, does not forget this sentence, *"It is extremely an unsatisfactory thing to voluntarily deprive oneself of immortality, as one who does not seek to have a wife and children."* I dare not say that every man should have a wife by his side, but on the contrary, I forbid it to many. I tell you that many occasions arise, by which the devil, the enemy of our tranquility, will come between a husband and wife, make the marriage unsuccessful, and bring many houses and families to ruin and decay.

William. I would be glad to know what those occasions are.

Anniball. Whoever wishes to make a narrow search for them, may find enough. I remember three of the most important, which should not be concealed in this discourse. The first is the inequality between spouses, either in age or in vocation, from which so many quarrels and inconveniences result, that it seems to me that the parties must be equal.

William. Touching on the age difference, I think it is an improper thing for a young woman to be paired with a man who has the appearance of being her father rather than her husband. I am convinced that young and pretty maidens go willingly to such husbands, as they would to their graves. They are sure to become widows during the lifetime of their husbands. Besides that, those who have been so matched know how troublesome an old husband is to a young wife. Yes, and worst of all, the poor souls are in this difficult situation, that, no matter how much honesty is in them or how much modesty is in their behavior, men will not refrain from murmuring that they are lewd and shallow, just because of their husband's white beards. I do not know which is more important, the husband's jealousy or the wife's suspicion.

Anniball. Consider, on the other hand, the good name that wrinkled and toothless women get by taking young and beardless boys as husbands, and tell me if the anger of those women is not greater than the hard fortune of the others. To make a long story short, there can be no agreement between such contrasts. Just as Venus and Saturn are constantly at war with each other, the old coupled with the young never agree. The same happens in marriages that are not equal in vocation and condition. As long as one has a noble soul and the other a vile disposition, there can be no consensus between them or agreement in goodwill, but continual quarrels and arguments.

Now, to the first cause of unhappiness in marriage, I will add the second, namely, when marriage is made against the will and liking of the parties. In this case, I have seen great inconveniences grow, with shame, blame, and belated repentance on the part of those who made them. This discontent is mostly on the part of the woman, without whose knowledge marriages are discussed and concluded, and dowries are said and paid. They are often transported by their husbands to unknown countries, among barbarous peoples, before they have any idea of the matter. In this way the wretched women, fearing the commandment and strictness of their parents, are often forced against their will and accept with their mouths what they reject with their hearts.

William. No such disturbances occur in France, where maids and men have the freedom to say yes or no, depending on their fancy.

Anniball. The third occasion is perhaps the most important and always produces negative effects, namely when a man takes a wife without a dowry.

William. You are right. When these husbands marry only for love and consider for themselves how their wives have brought nothing to them, their love begins to grow cold, and repenting of their folly, they begin to use them not as a wife but as a servant. While those who marry rich wives are assured that they still have something to be in love with, you see how nowadays beautiful women without wealth find more lovers than husbands. Few take wives for the love of God or, as they say, for their beautiful appearance. Every man now has his eyes open and cares not for flesh that has no taste or flavor, saying:

> *Bring something with you,*
> *if you want to live with me.*

Anniball. I see, sir, that you are mistaken in the matter, and have strayed far from my intent.

William. I beg your pardon.

Anniball. If a man marries a poor woman and makes her a slave, and a woman marries a poor man and makes him a slave, it all comes down to the same thing.

William. What you mean is a man should not take a wife that is richer or poorer, but equal in both, and should not take a dowry that is more or less.

Anniball. You still do not understand, because you consider the dowry as money.

Civil Conversation III

William. I believe that your interpretation of a woman's dowry is too obscure in terms. I would prefer to use the meaning according to the common interpretation, as you well know, which is commonly understood, based on the particular law enacted by the great legislator Lycurgus[1], that men marry women without a dowry.

Lycurgus of Sparta, By Merry-Joseph Blondel (1781-1853), 1828.

Anniball. Lycurgus gave this law to people composed of the learned and ignorant. He spoke in such a way that everyone could understand him. I speak to you because your depth of understanding can come to know the dowry that surpasses all others, which you are so abundantly endowed with, that if you were a woman, you would greatly enrich your husband.

William. Feeling pleasantly mocked by you, I understand, that you speak of the dowry of the mind.

Anniball. When Lycurgus was asked why he wished men to take wives without a dowry, he wisely answered that he did so with the intention that no one should be rejected because of their poverty, nor chosen because of their wealth. Since we live in a very different age from those times, it does not seem wrong that a dowry of a small amount should be taken to help bear the burdens of marriage and to support himself in his corresponding vocation. I wouldn't want someone to do as two old men in this town did, negotiating the marriage between the son of one and the daughter of the other. For five years, a hundred silver coins of the dowry were held back before concluding it, giving a clear indication to the world whether they were more desirous of parentage or robbery. Therefore, it is best to stay in the middle and marry someone who is neither too rich nor too poor. The poor brings into the other's house necessity and too rich brings servility. Since he who marries a poor woman is called thrice unhappy, there is also a common saying, *"Where dowry comes in freedom comes out."*[2] So, returning to where I began, one must beware of entering into marriage on a whim and allowing oneself to be carried away either by wealth or beauty without virtue. The same consideration should be given to women, who, are inclined often to fall in love with outward appearances, marrying someone, who is like a cypress tree, tall, and beautiful, but without fruit.

William. Since you allow the dowry to support the charge of marriage, I do not believe you would disregard the beauty of the wife for the contentment of the husband.

Anniball. Even if she is sufficiently attractive and endowed with a beautiful soul, nevertheless I would be loath to have for a companion someone I do not find attractive. Our nature abhors repugnant and unsightly things. Besides, an unattractive face is often taken as a sign of unfavorable conditions, and it seldom happens that a good mind is lodged in a homely body. If there is someone who, having seen their unsightliness in a mirror has made up for what the lack of nature provided with good qualities and virtue, though the wise regard them as beautiful and perfectly formed, the vulgar regard them as counterfeits. I remember a pretty

Marriage

good jest about a handsome gentleman who was married to a woman with a horrible countenance and an ugly face. He was invited to dinner by a gentleman of his acquaintance and arrived alone a little before dinner time. The mistress of the house thought he was a servant sent ahead before his master. Having already assigned duties to her servants requested the gentleman to chop some wood, which he did very diligently. The gentlemen who had invited him, having arrived in the meantime, asked him what he was doing. He replied with a cheerful demeanor that he bore the pain of his deformity. Therefore, you see how the bad favor of people diminishes their dignity. Just as I would not wish to have an ill-favored wife, neither would I wish to have one who is ill, or who is not likely to give birth to perfect and beautiful children. The more beautiful and well-proportioned the children are, the more amiable, fit for any undertaking, and able they are to obtain dignity and promotions. The poet Mantuan[3] promised by the mouth of Juno[4], a beautiful nymph in marriage to the King of the Winds so that he might become the father of beautiful offspring.

William. I believe that the most unfortunate husbands are those who are troubled with foul ill-favored wives, even if only in their dreams. I do not know which is worse, to have a poor wife or an unpleasant one.

Civil Conversation III

Anniball. Then you will know, which is worse, to live poorly, or to sleep badly.

William. It is quite true that the negatives of a poor wife are in a sense without remedy, while the inconvenience of a foul wife can be somehow remedied.

Anniball. In what way?

William. By providing a beautiful maiden for himself in his house, and doing as one said, I am not sure who:

*If someone has an ugly wife
and a wandering handmaid,
use this one, and it's enough to have the other.*

Anniball. This proverb comes from a wanton author, and it is rather to be reproved than followed. There was a gentleman in this country, who would not follow it in any way, whose happiness was to have a wife of great stature, with a rather long beard on her chin. A creature so monstrous in every way, that it was doubtful whether she was a woman or a tiger. To make a long story short, anyone that had to deal with her would rather do penance than commit offense. One day, while she was passing along the street in the company of some beautiful ladies, some gentlemen and strangers stopped to look at her, laughing and wondering about her. Her husband happened to pass by and one of them asked him what she was. The poor man, drawing back, said he did not know her.

William. He might as well say that he has more wives than he needed.

Anniball. Yet he had no more than he loved, because he used her well, and followed none of that corrupt advice you alleged now.

William. You tell me about the great goodness of a husband and the happiness of a wife. If he does not detest her, he at least does with her what men do with the things they take charge of, which is to keep them with great care, and never use them except in case of great necessity. As the proverb says, *"They do not love to be drunk with their own wine."*

Anniball. Well, as much as she is dear to him, he can be sure that she will not be taken away from him. Let's move on from the ugly to the beautiful.

William. A man cannot keep them safe, because everyone looks at them. I remember a gentleman sent a painter to the house of a very fair woman to draw her portrait, but her husband, who had arrived in the meantime, obstructed his work and threw him out the door. He told the painter that the gentlemen, who had sent him, after he had the copy, would try to have the original as well. In comparison, between the fair and the homely, I say for my part that it is less painful to be hung on a nice pair of gallows.

Civil Conversation III

Anniball. There is a common saying, "*He who has a white horse and a beautiful woman is never out of trouble.*" To which this question can be added, "*Did you take a beautiful wife to your detriment?*" You have often heard of various women whose singular beauty led their husbands to destruction. Moreover, we must remember that pride and beauty often go hand in hand. Herod's[5] wife, though sober and chaste, knowing the excellence of her beauty, became wonderfully proud and arrogant.

William. A poet demonstrated this, saying:

Her beauty is so evenly matched with pride,
that pleasing others is something she puts aside.

Anniball. Add to this that beauty breeds temptation, and temptation dishonor. It is almost impossible and rarely seen, that these two great enemies, beauty and honesty, get along. A man can hardly secure those things that almost all men desire and strive to achieve. Some attack them with their character, others with their good wit, some with the eloquence of words, and others with the magnificence of deeds. Even though it often happens that beauty and honesty are united, it seldom happens that exquisite beauty is suspected. Thus, the renown of the husband and wife is judged sinisterly. Permit me to speak of the wars and destruction of various people and countries, which occurred only because of the unparalleled beauty of some

Marriage

women. It will suffice to conclude that there is nothing in the world that causes more discord and trouble than a woman when she is desired by several men.

William. If a man cannot accept either fair or homely without incurring inconvenience, it is best not to meddle at all.

Anniball. Yes, you must take one that is neither fair nor homely. Long ago I learned that the perfection of the body consists of the right medium so that it is neither too strong nor too beautiful nor too weak nor too homely. One makes people bold and proud and the other weak and low-minded. Therefore, average beauty is highly valued and represents the best for a woman. Whereas the extremity of beauty or ugliness is disliked, one torments, and the other is loathed. In short, a woman's beauty, gestures, and countenances should be such that most men may like them because their husbands will be attracted to them and less apt to love others besides them. If they are not attractive to other men, surely their husbands will never think much of them, for a man does not care to possess what no man desires to have.

William. What do you think of those who enrich themselves with makeup, saying that they do it to please their husbands?

Anniball. Do you think that is the reason?

Civil Conversation III

William. I think the beautiful clothes they wear when they go abroad are more to please those who are abroad than the husband who is at home.

Anniball. We must also think that those who use artificial means displease God greatly, by altering his image, and do not please men than with an artificial painted beauty that shines more brilliantly. I wish those smeared, whitewashed, reddish-orange faces would consider what men scoff and jeer at when they are by themselves, given to those propped-up beauties, which are always accompanied by two false persuasions. First, they believe themselves beautiful by the force of those artificial colors, without knowing, as a poet says,

> *That painting could not make Hecuba[6] Helena[7].*

The other believes that those who look at them take this painting as a natural color. I once knew one who strongly complained about these counterfeit women. Yet, the poor fool could not perceive her dyed purple face where some colors blended with her head covering. These women would be judged in the same manner as many were once judged by an honest matron. While at a banquet, playing a game in which each, in turn, commands the others, when the matron's turn came, had a basin of water brought in with which she immediately washed her hands and face, commanding all the others to do likewise, so many of them in embarrassment and shame had their painted faces run down their cheeks. I also know a young lady, whose face two months ago was like a coal miner, and now she looks so bewitched, or rather so painted, that she seems quite like another woman. When she turns her head a little her neck and throat appear so black, so different from her face, one would say it was a Flemish head placed on the neck of a Moor.

William. Be that as it may, the poor woman does not know that the face paints described in the secrets of Alexis[8] will also work for the neck and throat.

Anniball. If such vanities are to be endured in women, one cannot forgive the gross folly of some husbands, seeing the painting of their wife; allow it, persuading them that it is done to please them. On the other hand, to please their wife, arrange their cap in the sharpest manner possible. Some husbands also find a lot of faults with those wives who do not like to curl their hair but comb it straight, swearing unceremoniously, if their wives did that, they would pull her neck back, like a hen. I don't know which one of these two kinds is the bigger fool, the one for loving what is bad, or the other for not loving what is good.

William. Truly I cannot think well of these women and assume that their colors are feigned, their hearts and affections false, so that no pure or faithful goodwill is to be expected from them. It is thought that love, being naked, does not like these false disguises. Therefore, our gentle Tuscan, should stop these curious follies, and give singular praise to Madam Laura[9] whose beauty qualifies as natural.

Young Woman ("Laura"). By Giorgine (1477 – Oct 25, 1510), 1506.

Anniball. We will therefore maintain that a

Marriage

woman who removes and changes the color and complexion that God has given her, appropriates what belongs to a harlot. Anything natural is the work of God; therefore, what is counterfeit is the work of the devil. Nevertheless, I must say that this type of art should not be generally condemned, but in some cases, tolerated. If a man is permitted to seek remedy to remove some wart, mole, spot, or similar misfortune that comes by chance, a woman should be permitted to correct by art any imperfection, whether natural or by chance, that appears on her face. For this reason, we deem it permissible for a woman to correct anything wrong with her using makeup if she is necessarily compelled to do so, either by some indisposition of her body, or for the preservation of her feminine state, provided that it is done so slightly and discreetly, that the artificial manipulation is not seen, or that is seen and is not disagreeable.

Since we agree that a wife should be chosen neither for beauty nor homeliness, it is best to go further and endow a wife with that dowry that can make the marriage firm and secure. First, we must reprove the abuse of men who, in choosing a wife, use no other order than what they use in buying a horse. The buyer will be sure to examine every part, whether it is the sound of wind and limbs, has no cracks or defects, is young and of good stature, has a good walk, and has those external marks which denote a good horse. I do not deny that by the appearance of a woman a man can form an idea of her character, but since God has commanded us not to judge by her face, we must use a more certain and convenient method.

William. I have always liked marriages that are treated openly, without hiding anything. Once something comes to light, it only brings grief and regrets to one of the parties. Neither men nor women use that order, endeavoring as much as they can to cover their faults, both of body and mind. Take the example of the painter who, while painting a one-eyed gentleman, would not paint his entire face, but would represent it in such a manner that the missing eye could not be perceived.

Anniball. This was not the case for the philosopher Crates[10], who, having been proposed marriage by a virtuous woman approached her, thinking that she did not know he had a crooked back, was lame, and poor, took off his cloak and placed it near his staff and wallet explaining to her that his wealth and looks were what was before her, and she needed to consider them well, lest she should later have reason to regret her proposal. For all this, she had no issue with him saying she could not have a richer or more handsome husband than him.

William. Now, please let's go to the point you

promised, where a husband can act confidently in their choice of a wife.

Anniball. The remedy is, to first ask God for a wife by prayer. Riches are given to us by the father and mother, but a wise wife is given to us by God. We should follow the authority of Olympia, mother of Alexander, whose word is worthy of being written in letters of gold, *"Women should be married first with the ears, then with the eyes."* Since the custom of our country does not allow men to practice freely in our homes, to keep ourselves familiar with the maidens that are to be married, as is the fashion in France and other places. We must at least procure with all our power from the mouths of many to our faithful ears, undoubted reports of their origin, life, and customs. The avarice of the world is such that asses, oxen, and horses (of good breed) are sought after, but the ill-born, vicious wife is not refused if she has plenty of money. The wise man will have a special regard for the conditions and qualities of his wife, and will note the life and conduct of her parents, remembering the sayings, *"The eagle is not born a dove,"* but *"The cat will always do what a cat will do."* In truth, it is very rare to see children deviate from the path of their parents and ancestors. I am sure you can recall families in which someone can see, by succession, in the nephews and children, the roots of greed, bestiality, foolishness, drunkenness, or other faults that their parents before them were tainted with. This verifies the proverb, "*A bad bird lays a bad egg,*" and on the other hand, "*It is rare that a good tree produces bad fruit.*"

William. I cannot agree with your opinion, because daily experience shows that this rule often fails, even though I cannot say that it is always false. If you search ancient history, you will note in a sense that nature does not play her part, for you will find many virtuous individuals that were raised by vile and foolish fathers. Conversely, many good and wise fathers had foolish and wicked children. If this is true, how can an honest woman have dishonest harlots for daughters? Therefore, we can assure ourselves that in marriage fortune has more influence than wisdom, and it is not enough to be so curious, to cross oneself, and be led blindfolded to this affair.

Anniball. The doubt you have raised is great and worthy of your ingenuity, but although it cannot be denied that good parents may sometimes have children of bad natures, that (as you say) my rule does not hold. Some say that it always happens that a good father has a wicked child which agrees with the saying, "*The children of princes and rulers are seldom as perfect as others.*" Yet they do not want nature to be at fault but assert on the contrary that nature does not do its duty when a wise father gets a son like himself. They base their opinion on some subtle philosophical reasons, which I intend to omit for now. Now, this being the case, it would be good for a man marrying to make sure that his wife came from bad parents, and it would be better for wise men to be careful how they marry, for fear of having foolish children. I do not believe this is the case, and therefore I answer you and those others that nature always tends to the best, so from good parents good children should naturally be born; and if sometimes the contrary should happen, nature is not to blame. Indeed, if you examine the matter carefully, you will see that in most cases this happens not by birth, but by education. This is why many coarse minds, through continuous study, become ready for use, while others, who in their cradle turn out to have a quick wit, in time, either through idleness, gluttony, or some other mismanagement, become slow and dull. Now, considering this, you can conclude that a father who, through much toil and trouble, both of mind and body, has gained riches and honors, even if his children have great intelligence, nevertheless is so overwhelmed with paternal affection for them, that knowing he has provided enough for them to live at ease, cannot bear to see their labor and toil as he has done. So, overcome by a certain tender affection, allows them to be brought up with delicacy and

Civil Conversation III

carelessness, and because of this laziness, their natural strength decays and, by habit and custom, turns to another nature. Consider, moreover, how children who feel so pampered and spoiled by their parents, keep themselves, as far as possible, away from the dust and sunshine. They do not care to apply their minds to anything worthy, nor try to get more than what their parents have left them; not unlike the crow, which lives only on the food that other animals leave behind. Certainly, there is no doubt that if they were raised modestly by their parents, they would become wise and sufficient. So you see, in most cases, children of the poor become rich through their study and industry, and the rich become poor through their neglect and laziness. This is signified to us by that pleasant wheel that turns this saying, *"Riches breed pride, pride poverty, poverty humility, humility riches, and riches again pride."*

We will therefore maintain for the truest and most touching generation that as man is made of men, and beasts of beasts, so from the good for the most part, good is created. A good father must be admonished not to trust so much in the goodness of his nature, as to think this alone is sufficient to keep his children good. Looking at them with a more well-advised, then pious and paternal eye, he should seek to improve their good nature, by exciting them to virtuous actions, making sure that to arrive at the

Marriage

perfection of virtue it is not enough to be well-born, but also to be well brought up. We will speak about this in a short while at a more appropriate time. In the meantime, in choosing a wife, it will do us no harm to inquire well into the honesty of the mother, in the hope that the daughter will follow her honest nature and conditions, and we will have much less difficulty in maintaining her in her goodness, than if, by the perverse nature of the mother, she were naturally inclined to evil.

It is not enough to know the qualities of the mother, but also to know the conditions of the father, because the children share the nature of both. It often happens that they derive from one some imperfection that the other is devoid of.

Although every man should have a wife from a good family, gentlemen should be especially careful to mate only with those who come from gentle blood. The Sophists[11] are very judgmental against the gentry, and they have no regard for the common things known to everyone, namely, to have good breeding. Men buy horses and dogs of good breed and also choose the best fruit. The Sophists do not consider it important for a gentleman's wife to be well-born for the children they will have between them. They do not weigh how much it matters to their children, whether their origin is barbarous or not. Being ignorant, they show they do not know that in a generation there are certain secret instincts of virtue and excellence, communicated from both parents to children.

William. Let's consider if it is true that education is another nature, it is not only necessary to know if the wife has been born of good parents, but also if she has been groomed and well-educated. This is rarely the case because there are some who, having only one daughter, are so blinded by the extreme love for her, they do not wish her to be hindered in her will in anything. Her parents allow her to live in all wanton pleasures and delicacy, which is then the cause of many inconveniences.

Anniball. You have not been deceived one iota. However, the husband should not be discouraged by the excessive tenderness towards her parents. Since she is still young, with the help of his good nature, he can easily, like a tender twig, straighten her out if she begins to become crooked, and with severe admonitions, reforms her disordered mind. From this, it may be inferred that it is better to marry a young girl than one that is mature in years, who is scarcely disposed to give up her old wicked ways if she has any.

William. Yet there are some contrary opinions, who believe that it is better to take a wife of a certain age and knows how to manage a home, than these infants who have just come out of the

Marriage

womb, whom you must either teach yourself or else appoint them a governor. Indeed, if a stranger came to my house that I wish to entertain, I would die of shame, if I had to deal with one of those simple underwater creatures, who can neither ask a question, nor give an answer, nor show herself a wise and gallant woman, and if she is unable to do so, I would rather lock her up and say that she is ill.

Anniball. You will never find a young woman so savory in every sense that she can please your taste, but living with you will change her ways and frame her to your liking. On this subject, if we consider how different the opinions of husbands are and how different the customs of countries are, we would linger too long here. Some are so kind-hearted that they want their wives to entertain their friends in their homes, considering themselves happy to have wives who can behave well in this respect. They are very glad that the world knows that in their house shines such a rare and precious pearl and jewel. Some, on the other hand, think it a disgrace that their wives are skilled in anything other than spinning and sowing. If strangers come to their house, they either run quickly themselves or send someone to warn their wife to withdraw, which they do, no different than the chicken when it sees a hawk coming. Compare the people of Siena to the people of

Rome, and consider how the Sienese, to do more honor to strangers in their home, make their wives present themselves as the dearest thing they have in the world. In contrast, the Romans impose on their wives a life so rigid that they look like cloistered nuns. In this diverse behavior, I will not provide any particular judgment. The custom of each country must be obeyed and must be observed as inviolably as a law. Nor do I wish to discuss which of the husbands do things better, those who show their wives off, or those who shut them up when their friends come to their house. Mary, I will say this, all of the honor and blame that may arise in either case, is not on the wives, but on the husbands, for they do nothing except what they are commanded to do.

Returning to the first point, a very young wife is easy to manipulate according to the pleasure of her husband. For a time her husband must willingly be her master (as you said) to direct her, yet it does him good to see that his precepts are easily followed, and he is proud that he has framed her (as they say) with his own hands and according to his own heart. I believe that it is considered a double pain to marry a widow because first, it is necessary to make her forget the qualities of her first husband, and then made to dance to the fiddle of the second.

William. In my opinion, these second marriages

taste like twice-soaked kale. They are all the more harmful if both parties have been married twice. It is told that while a husband and wife were having dinner together, the wife, despite her husband, gave half of the meat that was on the table to a poor man standing nearby, saying, *"I give this to you for the sake of my first husband."* The husband took the other half and gave it to him, saying, *"I give this to you for the sake of my first wife."* In the end, they both dined on dry bread.

Anniball. There is a worse disadvantage than this. This second marriage is very harmful to the children of the first marriage, who are tested by the cruelty of the stepmothers, who, receiving any blow or injury from their husbands, as soon as their backs are turned, take revenge on their children, beating them unmercifully in a very painful way that they cannot help themselves.

William. Sometimes the stepchild gets even, unwillingly, against the stepmother, while throwing a stone at a dog; it strikes her, saying, *"The blow was not altogether in vain."*

Anniball. I will also tell you that a man should choose a young woman rather than a middle-aged one. He should marry while he is young, and not wait until his hair turns gray. Since they are both young, they are more likely to have children; live to see them grow up, and in their older years enjoy their service and well-being, when the children can do as much for their parents as their parents did for them.

William. If I am not mistaken, all this talk is beside the point. So far we have been dilly-dallying in a discourse that has no other purpose than to teach a man to choose a young, well-born, well-mannered, reasonably wealthy, average-looking wife, of sound and robust constitution, and good wit and ability. We have yet to say a word about the manner of conversation between a husband and wife, as was our original purpose.

Anniball. I presuppose that to converse kindly with his wife, he must first be well-disposed to love her. Since a man cannot love perfectly what he does not know thoroughly, it is necessary first to learn to know (as we have done) the good qualities and conditions of one's wife, and what are the good parts in a woman, whereby men are induced to love them. Likewise, it is necessary for the father who loves his daughter, before she marries, to examine thoroughly the qualities, behavior, and life of his future son-in-law. It is true, *"When you have found a good son-in-law you have a good son, and if you find a bad one, casts away his daughter."* Now the husband, knowing the goodness of his wife, having to live with her, must above all love her with all his heart and without any plan, for so commands the law of God. This is the strong foundation that surely

Marriage

upholds marriage, and when neglected by the husband brings great shame and infamy upon him. If he does not love the one he has carefully and diligently found, and once deemed worthy of his love, clearly shows himself as a fickle and fanciful individual, and would be better off if he was matched with a jealous or spiteful woman, or some of the other furies, than a loving wife.

William. What does this love primarily consist of?

Anniball. In this, he is jealous of her love.

William. I think you are mistaken, for a woman would rather have her husband without love, than with jealousy?

Anniball. I do not speak of that jealousy which makes a husband doubt some false measure in his wife, but the fear that he will offend his wife in some way. You will understand better if you think of the jealousy with which you keep your prince's secrets locked up in your heart, constantly fearing that through your fault they will be discovered. In the same way, the husband must accompany his love with continual jealousy and fear, of losing by his fault the favor and goodwill of his wife, making sure that this is the only remedy that preserves that jealousy which makes the husband uneasy, which you referred to at the beginning. He cannot give his wife a surer sign of this sincere jealousy than by behaving to her as he would have her behave to him, and in so doing will be sure to find her so.

William. This is very good advice.

Anniball. Be assured, most of the faults committed by wives have their origin in the faults of husbands, who for the most part demand from their wives the exact observance of the laws of marriage, but they make no allowance for them. You will see some of them who, although they have received the company and comfort from women, in word and deed use such strictness towards them, and usurp such superiority over them, as is commonly used with slaves. If abroad they have received some injury, when they return home their wives are sure to suffer for it, proving themselves cowards towards others and good men towards their poor wives. It is no wonder that they are overcome with grief and rage, and call upon the devil to help them, and at that time some lewd fellows will have the occasion to try and subdue her and hope to overtake her because she is ready to follow whatever anger and despair have been put into her head. On the other hand, when the wife knows that all the rays of her husband's love, faith, and fidelity shine only on her, who is dearer to her than all other earthly things, you will see her consume herself in burning flames of love, and throw all her cares into thinking, and doing what she knows will please him. We reckon that a friend does not love his friend as much, a brother his brother, or a son his father, as a wife loves her husband, who not only conforms to his will but is completely transformed into him. Hence, arising between them, on both sides, such a security of trust and spirit that makes them live in marital bliss.

William. This assurance of confidence and peace of mind is not present in the hearts of all husbands, and I am convinced that there are very few in the world who, while putting on a good face, assure themselves of their wife's behavior.

Anniball. I believe you. Can you tell me where the common distrust men have for their wives come from?

William. Perhaps it is the frailty and weakness of the flesh that is attributed to most women.

Anniball. No, rather to the weakness of love, that is attributed to most men. Consider that at the door through which suspicion enters, love goes out. If by chance the husband has any occasion to distrust, let him examine his own life, and he will find that the occasion came because he did not treat her in the manner he should have. If he regrets it and begins to regard her as half of himself, and give her genuine affection, he will also begin to cast off suspicion and understand that he who loves is loved and that in mutual love an inviolable faith reigns.

William. A certain spirit tells me that this rule of yours is rather praised than practiced. Whoever wishes to observe it must leave the rope too loose on the woman's neck and entrust the care of her and her honor only to her little discretion. This, as you know, is not the custom of our country, Italy, where women are watched with the utmost diligence.

Anniball. A dishonest woman cannot be kept at home, and an honest one should not. Those who take it upon themselves to keep their wives honest think that the world will judge them better for it. They think that men laugh at those husbands who give their wives too much responsibility and convince themselves that if they do not keep them on a short leash, they do not keep them as they should. Moreover, they think that the wife, seeing that her husband does not care for her, will imagine that he does not care for her and convince herself that no one else wants her. Others, who do not restrict the freedom of their wives, persuade themselves that this is the way to keep them honest, alleging this reason that the wife, seeing her husband taking control of her honor, is dissatisfied with it, and no longer takes care to guard it. When her honor is entrusted to herself, she is careful and jealous of it, since it is hers. Besides, we naturally desire the things that are forbidden to us, and we know it.

She sins less, who has the free power to sin.

Indeed, she is considered honest only because having the freedom to do something wrong, she does not do it. To free ourselves from the oddities of these different opinions, I believe we must follow another way for it to work.

William. In what way?

Anniball. Don't you often see two porters carrying a load together?

William. Yes, absolutely.

Anniball. The husband and wife are two bodies supporting one mind and one honor so it is in their best interests for each of them to take care of their share of this common honor. They have to hold it upright because it is necessary to maintain such a measure of indifference that neither one has any greater burden than the other, but they leave each other their due share. They need to take special care that neither of them pulls to one side or the other. If one pulls back in any way, it is enough to make the cart fall into the quagmire. Therefore, to bear this honor bravely, there is nothing that will make them have better encouragement for each other, except to practice faithful and fervent love, once it begins to fail, whether, on one side or the other, this honor immediately falls to the ground.

William. Therefore, you are better off dividing this burden between the husband and wife and assigning their share.

Anniball. I will. As for the husband, he must know, just as Christ is the head of the man, the man is the head of the woman. Therefore, if he will follow his head in leading a Christian life, following the steps of our Savior and keeping his holy commandments, especially the inviolable bond of holy matrimony, there is no doubt that she will follow her head, as the shadow follows the body, and will take his ways and actions as the law of her life, and never forget them. If her husband changes his ways and his conditions, be assured that she will do the same, and follow the steps of Helen, who is said to have been chaste as long as her husband was content with her, and afterward abandoned herself to others, because of him. If he is a man of understanding, he will immediately realize that there is nothing more harmful, or infuriating to his wife, than the dishonest life of her husband. For not having faith in her, he must not expect her to keep her promise to him, as the proverb says, "*He who does not do what he must, does not receive what he expects.*"[12] I will tell you, according to the judgments of the wise, the adulterer deserves the most grievous punishment by how much he ought to surpass his wife in virtue and lead her by his example.

Additionally, the husband must consider what his authority is and to what extent it extends over his wife. Some of them hold their wives in such awe that they obey them not as a lord and master but as a tyrant, so much so that, turning love into fear, they make the poor women weary of their lives and eager to die. Whereupon, mistreating them, not without reason, they verify the proverb, "*When the husband makes earth of her, the wife makes flesh without him.*" The husband should not persuade himself that he is above his wife, as a prince over his subjects or the shepherd over his sheep, but as the mind over the body, which is bound together by a certain natural interest. Rather, consider that in the beginning, a man was not made of the woman, but the woman of the man, and she was taken, not from the head, so she might have dominion over the man, nor from the feet, so she might be trodden down by him, but from the side, where the heart lives, so he should love her with all his heart and as himself. According to the opinion of astrologers, the sun, which is lord of the stars, does not go about the firmament without the company of Mercury, so the husband, being Lord of the wife, must not exercise the authority he has over her without

Civil Conversation III

the company of wisdom. The husband should also provide for his wife's honest desires so that neither necessity nor indulgence drives her to dishonor. He should remember that both ease and sickness often make women immoral.

Many learned authors have laid down the husband's behavior towards his wife. It will suffice to say that, in order to bear righteously the burden of this common honor, he must regard his wife as his only treasure on earth and the most precious jewel he has. Therefore, he must take care that through his fault the price of her does not fall. He must also remember that there is nothing more due to his wife than the faithful, honest, and loving company of her husband. He must also allow himself, as a token of love, to communicate to her his thoughts and advice, for many have found much profit by following the advice of their wives, and a man is happy if he has a loving wife to whom he can communicate his good fortune, whose heartfelt joy doubles his joy. If he reveals any misfortune to her, she lightens his sorrow, by lovingly comforting him or helping him to bear some of it with patience.

If by chance he discovers any fault in his wife, either in words, gestures, or actions, he must reprehend her, not with reproach or anger, but as one who is mindful of her honor and others' opinion of her. This must always be done secretly between the two of them, remembering the saying, "*A man must neither chide nor play with his wife in the presence of others; for the one betrays her imperfections, the other his folly.*"

William. I certainly don't like those who still poke fun at their wives in front of others, because this sets other men's teeth chattering and make their wives ashamed and modest.

Anniball. Just as one should not like this, one should not like the scowling attitude of a farmer toward his wife. It makes others feel sorry for the hard life she leads with him, so much, they seek the most agreeable remedies they can. That is why I would like them to always be gentle and kind to their wives, both in word and deed, without making fun of the reason that it is claimed that some women love their lovers better than their husbands. It is that the lover, in the presence of his lady, is very careful about his behavior, not to use improper gestures, but makes sure that all his gestures and attitudes are as amiable as possible. The husband does not do this, being with her every day, and does not care about what dirty jokes he plays on her, which no doubt makes her like him less. He must therefore think that his wife being of a delicate nature, seeing in him such gross incivility, not only abhors it but begins to think that other men are more discreet and better bred than he. Thus, it behooves him to correct and modify his behavior; otherwise, he offends the decent thoughts of his wife. He must conform, to all honest and reasonable things, and beware of anything that may displease her. This way he will earn the praise, that the men of old attributed to good husbands, esteeming them more than good governors of countries.

William. Now let's discuss, if you please, how the wife should behave.

Anniball. The wife has two major disadvantages in maintaining this common honor. The first is that if the divine law commands the husband to love his wife, the same law commands the wife not only to love her spouse but also to be submissive and obedient to him. Therefore, it must be made clear to them that the wise matrons of old, particularly Sarah[13], called her husband lord and master.

William. These women have all the more advantage and good fortune, when their husbands obey them, submitting to their command.

Anniball. This is a term that refers rather to misfortune and bad luck. These husbands are mostly fools, dolts, weak, asinine, beastly, and are commonly called "*wittols*[14]." They believe so strongly, that they convince themselves that nothing bad is happening, even if they see another man with their wife in bed together.

Hence, their foolish wife, like a headless body, goes astray. Even if they have discretion and good sense, the world takes no notice of them. On the contrary, the husband's wisdom, valor, and authority serve to defend the honor of his wife, who thereby enjoys a greater reputation.

William. Yet you see that women are happy to meet gentle-natured, somewhat foolish men, so they can keep them under their control.

Anniball. Those who prefer to command over the foolish than obey the wise, are like those who prefer to lead a blind man on the road, rather than follow another with perfect sight and know the direct path they should take. These women do not have to boast of their sufficiency, because today the race of the Spartan women is worn out, and so they should be content to let their husbands wear the pants.

William. A man may easily give women this good advice, but few will follow it and still not seek to be in charge of their husbands.

Anniball. It is reasonable and by nature that the stronger should command over the weaker, but some women have the art of ordering things so well that their husbands are thought to do wrong if they arrange them otherwise. Whereupon Cato[15] used to say to the Romans, *"We command over the whole world, and our wives command over us."* There is no doubt that many

Civil Conversation III

rulers of cities and countries are dominated by their wives. Those women know there is a time and place to be obedient to their husbands. There are some so restless and resistant to authority, they never allow themselves to be commanded. By their importunities, exclamations, reproaches, and brawls, they continually oppose the will of their husbands and mock them, playing a thousand tricks on them, which made a certain king say, "*They were fools who followed their wife while running away from them.*"

William. You bring to mind that husband, whose wife had drowned in a river, went weeping along the river bank looking for her against the current, and was told that there was no doubt she had gone down with the current. "*Alas,*" he said, "*I cannot believe it, she did everything in her life against the current, so now in her death she surely must have gone against the current.*"

Anniball. We will therefore say that the wife, as the weaker person, must obey her husband. Just as men must observe and abide by the laws and statutes of the country, women must fulfill the commandments of their husbands, thus becoming the masters of the home. I have heard of several virtuous women who, by clothing themselves in humility, caused their husbands to abandon pride, cruelty, and other noteworthy vices. Some confess that they have forgiven their enemies and withdrawn their hands from taking revenge. Others have undone illicit deals, and still, others have abandoned blasphemy and other vanities. They have impassioned themselves to devotion and the health of their souls convinced and led to this by the sincere and honest prayers, good example, and humble Christian life of their wife.

William. Now that you have spoken about the wife's first disadvantage, can we please move on to the second?

Anniball. The second is, if she sees her husband backsliding under her burden and failing in the love and fidelity he owes her, she must not do as he does, but virtuously make up for his shortcomings. She will have to show to the world, for her part, she did not consent to this common honor being violated, but rather reckoning it is her part to bear the whole cross alone. In doing so, she will have double the reward from God and double the praise from the world. Therefore, we can deduce that this honor depends more on the diligence and faithfulness of the wife than the husband. Even if the husband offends God as much as the wife, violating the sacred bond of marriage, the wife must firmly impress it upon her heart and always remember that the husband because of his own fault, according to the opinion of others, stains his honor only a little. The wife will lose her good name altogether and is stained with such infamy that she can never again recover her honor either by repentance or the amendment of her life. Therefore, a wise woman should plug her ears against the charms of those who lie in wait for her chastity and open her eyes to this sentence,

A woman who lets herself be deprived of her honor, is no longer a woman, nor is she alive.

To keep her honest, both in deeds and in name as much as she can, she needs to avoid women who have a bad reputation. Women who endeavor by their naughty fashions and dishonest language lead others to do as they do, and wish with all their hearts that all women should be like them. The wife should know that to keep the law to which she is bound, it is not enough, to be honest, and innocent in deeds, if she does not also avoid all suspicion of dishonesty. If she takes a good look at the matter, she will find little difference (concerning the world) between being bad and being thought so. Therefore, a discreet woman will flee from all levity and vanity, and keep herself (out of the fire) from giving the slightest suspicion to her husband or others in the world, knowing that if a woman's chastity is suspected, lives in this world in a miserable state. When she hears bad things said about other women she needs to

Marriage

contemplate, imagining to herself that when a woman has achieved a bad reputation, whether deserved or not, it will take a lot to regain her honor. She should not lean so boldly on her honesty, thinking that God will always keep his hand on her head. He often allows a woman to be unjustly accused to punish her levity and vanity, where she has had occasional scandals and offenses.

William. I grant you that there are women who, feeling themselves loved by their husbands and taking special care of their honor, stay honest. I would like you to name me one woman who is the miracle of her sex, and despite all her honesty, does not show the world some sign of levity and vanity, and who is not content to be courted and be taken as beautiful. She also does not act courageous and happy in keeping her suitors in suspense for a long time between yes and no, and she does not think by these means to increase her reputation.

Anniball. It is as common for women to be vain and light as for peacocks to spread their tails. We should not wonder what someone once said, *"When we have taken away all vanity from a woman, a man cannot take anything else from her."* Why do you think women are so happy to be courted, intending not to yield, but to remain true to their honesty?

William. I am not content to know that I am an

Civil Conversation III

honest man unless the world knows it too. Women are moved by the same ambition and love to be courted and tested so that by their honest answers they may be recognized by the world as honest women.

Anniball. These same women move with a purpose, similar to those men who intimidate and bully others, who start fights to show how ferocious and mean they can be. These men put themselves at risk most of the time and in the end, are beaten up so badly that they end up in the hospital. The petty women trust their minds with that love to quarrel, but in the end pull the Devil's ears so much, allowing them to be pulled so far that they can no longer return to their calm selves. They find themselves led to a less pitiful and worse place than a hospital. If they happen to come out victorious, the world will doubt their honesty.

You did not mention that some women love to be subservient to their lovers. They put on a show with jewelry and other ornaments, putting their servants and suitors on their guard to confuse other women, so they may still be seen as well esteemed by their beauty and good grace, deserving to be loved.

William. Those women in my mind will pluck out one of their own eyes just so they can pluck out two from other women.

Anniball. We have spoken about two instances

Marriage

of their vanity, so now it is time to discuss two colorful excuses which they cover up this fault. Some say that God knows how much harm they can do with these amorous fools and how much he abhors them. Their presumption and insolence are so great, that they love a woman despite herself, and are so afraid of her that they dare not appear at doors or windows unless she comes to them.

William. It would be better if they never went around justifying themselves than to do it in that way, for it is a well-known fact that no man is such an ass. The continual laughter and rejection will make him flee. Instead of their smiling faces, eager looks, surrendering gestures, and other lewd tricks they show a serious look, demure face, modest gestures, and behavior befitting an honest woman. You would soon see these pigeons abandon the dove house.

Anniball. Others use a different excuse and say, as in an act of confession, to get their husbands away from the company of other women and lure them back home, they are inclined to let these amorous fellows follow them.

William. I can tell you that these women take it upon themselves to make their husbands do exactly what they do not want them to do, and like some physicians, make work when everything is perfectly fine.

Anniball. We will therefore briefly summarize

the sum of what we have said and admonish the wife when chastity is joined with vanity which is hardly worthy of praise. It rather lends itself to the words of King Demetrius[16] when he heard a married man criticize one of his concubines, and said to him, "*My concubine is far more modest than your Penelope.*" A woman must be careful not to give men occasion to think badly of her either by her actions, appearance, words, or clothing.

William. Since you mention clothing, I cannot fail to mention the abuse that is being committed nowadays in our country concerning the fashions and adornments of women. They spend all of their husband's money, on their clothing and accessories, the entire dowry they have brought with them, which truly astonishes me. What appalls me the most is to see husbands not only consent to this excessive burden, but also to the remarkable vanity their wives display in dressing themselves lasciviously like prostitutes, causing men to laugh at them, rather than admire them. After you left yesterday, I saw some women, one who had her braids crossed in such a way on her head that they made the figure of two hearts tied together. From there departed two branches of carnation silk, like two darts. Around the hearts, between the braids, were tied knots of silk and hair, representing amorous passion. From the crown of her head hung a label that fluttered in the wind, signifying her lightness and unfaithfulness. On her forehead, the hair made the shape of a garland, which was adorned with pearls and jewels, and with natural and artificial flowers, in such variety that the gardens of Naples are unable to produce more types. I will not mention a thousand other trifles, which have clouded and dazzled my eyes, as certain maps do, where the squadrons of men on horseback, the troops of men on foot, and the number of artillery pieces are drawn in small figures. Please tell me, are all these additions made by wives to please their husbands?

Anniball. Such a beautiful feat lacks only a motto in golden words.

William. What are these mottoes?

Anniball. *Offense to God, hope to the amorous, and destruction to their husbands.*

William. I do not see how men can maintain their wives in such a pompous and masked manner except to lend their money with exorbitant interest rates and use other deceitful methods.

Anniball. I will not say that they keep their wives so brave through deception and fierce bargaining. They live very poorly, barely supporting themselves, purging the sin of pride by abstinence of the mouth, and starving their children to death.

Although women are very curious about all their

attire, it is their hair that they spend the most time on. There is no kind of ointments and ground sauces that they will not try to make their hair the most magnificent color. Many have altered the color of their hair through such dangerous methods only to cause their own death. Their foolishness is so great, even though by such deceptions, they feel their heads hurt and their brains go haywire. As murderers of themselves, they do not want to give up this shameful and deadly practice. If they knew what women's appreciation and reputation consist of, you know they would not stay up most of the night and get up early in the morning to devote most of the day to styling their hair. They would conclude that those who do the least are cared for better, as the saying goes, "*Less is best.*"

William. I have always thought that women whose minds are not adorned with virtue and goodness are the ones who go to greater lengths than others to make up for this by adorning their bodies. Thinking that they have the same good fortune as the lapwing, which, although a vile bird living mostly in dirty lakes, was honored more than the other birds at the eagle's wedding because of the crown or crest on her head with her colorful feathers.

Anniball. It often happens that they do the opposite. The multitude of ornaments cover up what little good there is in them by nature, and

Marriage

the glitter of their jewels obscure the splendor of their virtues, especially if they weakly shine with little intensity, as they do in such women. It is usually seen that women, though never so honest, are not satisfied with such trifles. Therefore, it is said, *"At mills, women always lack something."*

Some show this insatiable desire not only in life, but also in death. You can find in her last will where she requests to be buried with her pearls and emeralds that she wore for her adornment. On the contrary, the wife of an emperor was greatly praised, since she never wished to wear clothing or jewels more precious than those worn by other women. She did this so as not to provide an example of vanity or pride. If honest women would reflect on the matter, they would see that it is not the golden bridle that makes the horse better, and because of these affected follies, their honesty is suspicious. This is demonstrated by the words of a poet, who rebuked an honest woman who committed this folly, comparing her to her lascivious sister in this respect.

Your sister seems chaste, for wearing chaste attire,
although her unchaste life has sunk
her chaste name in the mire.
You are a harlot[17] if a man should do you wrong,
but it is certain that it is a harlot
your clothes belong to.

I will also tell you that civil law states that if a man mistreats an honest matron, dressed like a harlot, there is no remedy against him by law. Therefore, women should be careful to dress so modestly, that they please their husbands, instead of making them jealous by dressing scantily. They must consider that men think that in a gorgeous body, a vain and useless mind is lodged.

William. I have often noticed that ladies who are so curious in their attire, are very wanton in their homes, and others who neglect this folly, are very good housewives.

Anniball. There is a common saying, *"You can't drink and whistle at the same time."* It is no wonder that those who spend all day deceiving themselves have no care or free time to see their house well-ordered. Let us put an end to this matter by concluding that it can be rightly said about these expensively lined carcasses that the feathers are worth more than the bird.

William. I think we should return to the matter from which I diverted you with my digression.

Anniball. I will be brief and give instructions to the wife to not only avoid what may anger and displease her husband but to also endeavor to do what pleases him. Just as a mirror makes a sad face seem joyful or a joyful one sad is worth nothing. The woman is a fool who, seeing her husband cheerful, pouts, or gets angry, or seeing him thoughtful, shows her to be agreeable. Therefore, she should resolve to conform to her husband's thoughts and judge things as sweet or sour, according to his taste. Where there is a diversity of minds and manners, love and goodwill will rarely last. Let her through sweet words and loving acts show him all the signs of affection she can. Considering that some husbands, accustomed to the amorous courtesies of other women, do not think their wives care for them if they do not show them similar or greater signs. In any case, she should continue to show her normal kindness to him, or she may seem to grow cold and appear to have committed some crime, putting a foolish idea into his head. If he possesses this idea, she must endeavor by all possible means to help him get rid of it. Some foolish women, with great indiscretion and to their detriment, seek to maintain that suspicion in their husbands so others will lay siege to their chastity.

William. Do you think these women are right to let their husbands know when they are bothered by unlawful requests?

Anniball. Those women are commonly blamed because much harm usually follows.

William. Should they not show their fidelity so their husband may have security?

Anniball. I think it is a poorly done thing, because it does not create peace of mind, but problems for the husband causing him doubt because if he does not reveal one love, he hides another. The worst thing is it gives rise to a quarrel between the husband and the lover, from which a good amount of mischief can ensue.

William. We love others well, but we love ourselves better. It would be better for her to endanger others rather than herself because she has reason to doubt that her husband does not learn about it through other means, and so he might think badly of her for keeping it from him.

Anniball. A wise woman will always prefer her husband to know through the report of others, the repulsion she has for her lover, rather than boast of her honesty herself. A wise husband

Marriage

will be more content with this and will be sure in his mind of his wife's honesty.

William. Many would think otherwise and do not agree with this interpretation of concealment.

Anniball. This is true, and so to avoid this problem, an honest woman should be so sober and chaste in her appearance that no man can be so bold to assault her. Indeed, when garrison's come to parley they are at the point of surrender. On the other hand, if she happens to be attacked, answers her lover as a virtuous lady did, *"When I was a maiden, I was at the disposal of my parents, but now that I am married, I am at the disposal of my husband. So, you had better speak to him and find out what he thinks I am going to do."* If her husband is away, she should remember to always act as if he were present and to show him, when he returns, the amount of work she has been doing in the house during his absence. This way, she will be more appreciated and praised by him.

William. To tell the truth, a wise husband will derive great pleasure from these things. Some are so fussy and brazen that they are never satisfied with anything their wives can do, but resent them so much that they wish to leave this world. I wish you would teach those poor souls some remedy for this horrible way to act.

Anniball. I have already indicated the remedy

Civil Conversation III

when I advised them to be obedient to their husbands. I also add, following the example of the physician, she must try to cure her husband's illnesses with contrary medicines. Therefore, if he is rough and terrible, she must overcome him with humility. If he chides, she must keep silent, for the answer of wise women is silence, and she must remain to tell him what she thinks until he is appeased. If he is obstinate, do not object too much and do not do as this woman did, when her husband brought two thrushes for dinner, she maintained that they were owls or blackbirds. He replied that they were thrushes, and she maintained that they were not; at that point, he became angry and gave her a smack on the ear. Yet, when the thrushes were served at the table, she continued to call them owls, so her husband began to smack her again. A week later, she brought the owls back to his mind and continued to persist; her husband was forced to start again with his old remedy. The matter did not end there and at the end of the year, she hit him in the mouth, because he had beaten her for two owls. He snapped back that it was for two thrushes, but she replied that he had deceived himself. And again, she was beaten for it one more time.

William. What do you think of those husbands who beat their wives?

Anniball. The same as I do sacrilegious people

and church robbers.

William. I remember reading a verse, but I do not remember from where,

> *A woman, an ass, and a walnut tree,*
> *Bear more fruit, the more they are beaten.*[18]

Anniball. You remember the text, but not the problem it represents, which is,

> *He offends God and undoes holy love,*
> *who strikes his wife with violent blows.*

William. Yet, in the opinion of a wise author, a man makes his wife better by chastising her.

Anniball. That author has no authority on the matter, for he immediately adds, "*A man bearing it, makes himself better.*"

William. Why, can a man not beat his wife on a just occasion?

Anniball. You say on a just occasion, but the man who restrains himself for that occasion will never beat his wife because a man should never need to beat his wife.

William. Yes, but can a man beat her if she commits any fault?

Anniball. If she commits a fault, through my fault, I am more worthy of being beaten than she is, but if she commits it through negligence, how can I in my heart even touch a hair on her head? If she does it willfully, I should rebuke her with

Civil Conversation III

words and attempt to reform her with good counsel. I should explain to her the shame of what she does wrong, and praise what she does right. If that does not help, I should bear with her patiently rather than beat her sternly. I must consider that she is a weak vessel, and we who are strong must tolerate the infirmities of the weak. I must consider that she is the flesh of my flesh, and no one has ever hated or hindered his own flesh, and must consider that we must be comforters of one another. Should I become her tormentor? With what face can I embrace that body my hands have bruised and battered? With what heart can she love the man who finds it in his heart to beat her?

William. Well, I perceive that you will be a loving husband. Let's move on and tell me if there is anything else on the part of the wife that will help her to maintain the love and goodwill between her husband and herself, and keep intact the common honor that we have spoken about.

Anniball. A woman cannot do anything to make her husband more in love with her. Not only does it do him good to see his wife so thrifty, but he forms an opinion of her honesty. He sees her take care of and exercise her body in the housework, whereby she obtains a lively natural color that falls off neither by sweat, weeping, blowing, nor washing. This causes him not to

Marriage

deny her any belonging to the home when he sees her being so careful in keeping it in good order. This is not the fashion of those light housewives who do nothing including caring for the husband, children, or anything belonging to the home. These women demonstrate that although the body is at home the mind is abroad. They are ashamed of them and are a disadvantage to their husbands. It is well-known that when the mistress is occupied in vanities the servants care little for her profit, but look to their own affairs. As some common sayings go, *"While the mistress plays, the maid strays,"* and *"While the cat's away the mice will play."*

Just as the wife must look around in her house, it is improper for the husband to meddle in the affairs within the home. If it is his fate to have a foolish wife who sleeps (as they say) with her eyes open. Know that it is up to him to make up for his wife's imperfection. Those men should be mocked who, having wise and sufficient wives, (as it is said) put the chickens out, season the pot, dress the meat, instruct the maids, and take away from their wives their duties. These husbands greatly offend their wives, showing they either distrust them or despise them. Moreover, they wrong themselves and show that they are up to no good. If they were engaged abroad in essential affairs, belonging to discreet men, when they returned home they would be

Civil Conversation III

more eager to rest than disturb their wives and servants by meddling in their affairs. They would consider that the management of the home belongs to the wife. God made women more fearful than men to be better suited to watch over and guard the home where careful fear is very necessary. I do not deny that the husband should know how things are going on in his home, provide for things accordingly, and, from time to time, correct some faults which, perhaps, will not or cannot do. It is reasonable that since she is, as it were, the manager of the home the husband should entrust to her the entire administration of it, as a thing that belongs to her.

You should know that through adversity and hardship, true friends are known. A wife cannot maintain goodwill between her and her spouse, and bind them, as it were, to her forever, except by remaining faithful to him in his need and adversity. Some of them do not do this, yet gladly participate in their husbands' prosperity and joys, but do not willingly participate in their hardships. Let's not forget the example of the beautiful and wise wife of Mithridates[19] (Hypsicratea[20]), because she loved her husband, cut her hair, prepared herself to ride, and wore armor like a man. She valiantly, faithfully, and patiently accompanied him through all his hardships and dangers. This gave Mithridates

Marriage

Detail of a miniature of Mithridates VI and his wife, Hypsicratea, on horseback. France, Central (Paris)

wonderful comfort in his adversities and showed the world that there is nothing so troublesome and grievous when the hearts of a husband and wife are united together and can support it. Therefore, when husbands are afflicted with some infirmity of mind or body, the wives should be ready, both in word and deed, to comfort and assist them. This way they will see their love and affection become more fervent and faithful.

In conclusion, the husband and wife should consider all things in common with each other, having nothing of their own in particular, not even their bodies. They should put aside pride and cheerfully put their efforts into choosing things to do in the home, which belong to their calling and strive to help each other in doing well. Hence, they will grow a contented tranquility, which will happily prolong their lives to old age. Through this bond of love and peaceful coexistence, they will set an example for their children to live in unity with one another, and for their servants to agree in the conduct of their affairs and the performance of their duties.

Parents and children

William. Since you have mentioned children, let's discuss the conversation between parents and children. I think it is very important to lay down the rules that they should observe in conversing with one another, since among them there is not, for the most part, a good agreement and discreet behavior that there should be. The world has now come to the point that a child does not have time to understand anything before he begins to think about the death of his father. Take the example of a child riding behind his father who simply says to him, *"Father, when you are dead, I will ride in the saddle."* Many clever children desire and plan the death of their fathers. I am not sure who is to blame, whether it is the parents, who do not hold their children in awe and educate them as they should, or the children, who do not know how much they owe to their parents.

Anniball. Which of them is ultimately at fault?

William. The child of course. They cannot bring action against their parents, even when they have been harmed by them.

Anniball. Why did you not say that the child is often ignorant of their duties to their parents?

William. I did say that.

Anniball. Who will you give the task of making the child know and understand their duty?

William. The parents.

Anniball. Then you should revoke your first sentence and conclude that the fault lies with the parent, who ought to have informed them of their duty.

William. If the parent gives good instruction to the child, but they do not listen, what more can they do? If the parent offers instructions with the right hand, and the child receives them with the left hand, where did the parent fail?

Anniball. When the parent teaches them to use their right hand, they will never become left-handed. It is not surprising that after having let them use this bad habit for a long time, it cannot be taken away. Therefore, the blame is their negligence for waiting until evening to give them instructions that should have been given in

Parents and children

the morning at sunrise, together with the nurse's milk, without considering that in tender minds, as in wax, a parent can make any impression they like.

William. I don't know how you can excuse children who, after their parents have carefully nurtured and educated them under the guidance of learned men and instructed them in the faith of Christ, eventually go astray, live lasciviously, and produce fruit unworthy of their good upbringing.

Anniball. This rarely happens and even if it does, parents are not exempt from the care that God himself has entrusted to them.

William. I am not surprised that a virtuously brought up child sometimes falls into disgrace or that discord arises afterward between his father and him because their diversity of morals cannot be the cause. It seems strange to me, as if it were against nature, that both father and son being upright men and because of their good behavior, well regarded by all men, often find themselves unable to agree at home and living in continual dispute and dissension. They agree in public affairs, yet disagree in domestic affairs. I could give you numerous examples of this behavior.

Anniball. You said earlier that a son should not bring an action against his father. If you want to abide by that point, you must confess that the son, however honest he may be, does not act honestly when he opposes the father and does not comply with his will.

William. I acknowledge that the son must allow himself to be commanded by his father and obey him without resistance. For their conversation to improve, the father must proceed in his paternal jurisdiction. In doing so he does not overstep the bounds of reason and give the son cause to find him at fault in his heart and to think he is mistreated by him, whereby the love and reverence he should bear his father is cooled and weakened.

Anniball. I can never forget the undeniable adage, *"Few sons, indeed, are like their fathers. Generally, they are worse; but just a few are better."*[21] Therefore, I would first like to look for the cause of why very few sons are like their father, explain the expectations that he has for them, and explain where the disagreement between them arises. This way we will better understand what their conversation should be.

William. Please continue.

Anniball. First, consider that children bring little or no comfort to their parents if nature and fortune are not tempered well in them.

William. How so?

Anniball. Just as a fruitful grain sown in

Parents and children

unsuitable soil yields no fruit, a child who is naturally inclined to learn will never do well if he is allowed to wage war. This is so true that you must know from the start what his inclination is. Touching on this subject, I remember reading some verses from Dante that I have forgotten.

William. I believe I may be able to help you here.

Anniball. That would be great.

William.

> *If the world below would fix its mind*
> *on the foundations laid by nature,*
> *in pursuing this, the people would be good.*
> *But you set aside for religion*
> *the one who was born for war,*
> *and you make a king of the one who is made for sermons,*
> *therefore your steps wander from the road.*[22]

Anniball. What a pleasure these verses give me, both because of their delightful harmony and because they make me realize how good a memory you are endowed with. You see here expressed one of the occasions of the unfortunate success of children.

William. It is in the best interest of the parents to use discretion on this point, to discover, one way or another, the natural instincts of their children. This is best known in their childhood,

Civil Conversation III

as the proverb says, *"From the morning you know a good day."* Although this matter of respect is very necessary, most fathers pay very little attention to it, forcing their children to enter into a professional life that is contrary to their natural inclination. It is no wonder that they receive little comfort from them. It often results in the dishonor of their house, and what is worse, a great offense to God. Take the example of when poor girls who, from their mother's womb, desired to be married are put into convents.

Anniball. Those parents who put their children into things contrary to their disposition should be pitied rather than blamed, for this commonly happens because they are not paying attention. Those who push them into religious houses before they are old enough to choose or refuse that life undoubtedly and greatly bear the blame because they bring their children there either through fear or through false persuasions. This is nothing else than opposing the will of God and taking away from their children that free choice that he has promised them in his divine goodness. Therefore, if the parents care about the honor and tranquility of their home, they must also be careful to know whether the minds of their children are inclined to learning, arms, agriculture, or merchandise. If they find that they have led them astray from the right path, they need to immediately guide them to the correct path, otherwise, be assured that something that begins badly will end worse.

William. If we want to find the cause of why children often do not develop according to the hope and opinion of their parents, we must begin with the milk the children drink. Since the milk from the nurses is so much stronger, the child bonds to the nurse rather than the mother who brought them into the world. I remember the custom of various women in France, who bring up their children with milk from animals. I think this causes the ferocity in many of them and they lack that reasonable part that is proper to men, which is said to always save their gratitude.

Anniball. There is no doubt about the wonderful effects of milk, and it is a very certain thing that if a lamb is fed with the milk of a goat or a kid with the milk of a sheep, the kid will have the softest hair and the lamb coarse and hairy wool. Therefore, it must be thought that the child, because of the milk, takes on the complexion of the nurse and the disposition of the mind follows the complexion of the body. It also happens that the daughters of honest women prove altogether dissimilar to them, both in body and in mind. So, to deliver children from their mothers to the nurses is nothing more than a corruption of nature.

If we were to mention this first nurture we should have done so when we discussed unfortunate marriages. I did not speak of it then nor will I do so here because the philosophers, and particularly Galen[23], have spoken so pertinently and sufficiently of the power and virtue of milk that we do not need to ask any more questions about it. I have also refrained from speaking about it because women of today are so concerned with their beauty or rather their vanity. They prefer to pervert the nature of their children rather than change the shape of their firm, hard, round breasts. Hence, it follows that the children, adapting themselves to the moods of their nurturers, turn away from the love and duty they owe to their mothers. They lack the blood in them to obey or respect anything which can be shown by the example of the bastard from the house of Gracchi. When he returned from war laden with the spoils of the enemy, he had his mother and his nurse come before him. He gave his mother a silver ring and his nurse a gold necklace. When his mother was displeased he said to her that she was wrong to do so saying, *"You carried me only nine months in your belly, but my nurse kept me at her breast for two years. What I have from you is my body which you hardly gave me honestly, but what I have from her proceeds from pure and sincere affection. Once I was born you deprived me of your company and banished me from your presence, but she graciously received me, disappearing into her arms, and raised me so well, that she brought me to what you see."* These reasons, together with others that I will not repeat, shut the mother's mouth who, was very ashamed and made his beloved nurse fall even more in love with him.

William. Since these women will not be the mothers of their children, they should at least take care to choose good nurses and good complexions.

Anniball. As the first abuse creeps in, putting their children in the care of a nurse, it follows that the second does not respect the nature of the nurse. Let us proceed to show the differences between fathers and their children, demonstrating with certainty that the principal one proceeds, as we have already indicated, from the difference between the nature of the child and the seat and profession of life to which they are destined. Therefore, I say that it is not enough for the father to know where the child is naturally destined if they do not endeavor to make the way easy for them, to assist them, and to pay attention to all that is necessary to lead them safely to their intended destination.

Another cause of this difference between the father and the child is when the father loves himself more than the child, keeping them with him to play with, without bothering to entrust them to masters to instruct them in learning, or to the court, or to the professions for which they are best suited. In this sense, many wealthy fathers make grave mistakes because leveraging their wealth, they never bother to educate their children in learning and virtue, but let their wits be dulled to such a degree by idleness and greed, they do not know the difference between *chaff and corn, chalk and cheese,* or *apples and oranges.* They grow up to have judgment like an ass, who judged the song of cuckoos to be sweeter than the song of nightingales.

William. The more the father keeps his children around them, the more they begin to resemble him.

Anniball. You are mistaken, for the life of the old father is not a model for the young son to model his actions after. In time, he will blame his father for denying him the opportunity to go abroad to gain wealth and esteem, because he kept him at home, thus preventing his advancement.

William. The child should rather think well of him for this, and attribute it to too much love.

Anniball. No, rather too little love. Inordinate

Parents and children

affection is not considered true love.

William. The dearer a thing is to you the more care you take to keep it around you and to join it, as it were, to your heart.

Anniball. True. But let me ask you, why do you wish to keep a good servant around for a long time?

William. For my profit.

Anniball. If he were called by some prince, to some higher rank, would you not permit him to depart from you?

William. Yes, gladly.

Anniball. Why?

William. For his advancement.

Anniball. Then you give him a greater sign of goodwill by letting him leave than by keeping him with you. In this way, you prefer his profit before your own. For the same reason, the father who keeps his child with him shows that he loves himself more than his child. If he loved him as he should, he would also love his advancement and seek to improve his estate. He would rather see his child die like a horse in battle than live like a pig in the mud.

William. What would you say if the father, being learned, kept his son with him so he can partake in his knowledge?

Civil Conversation III

Anniball. I have not mentioned such fathers, for there are very few who are endowed with sufficient knowledge to accomplish such a matter. If there are any, they are unwilling or unable to take such pains, nor to bind themselves to such an endeavor, having other business to attend to. If they did, there is no doubt that great good would come from it because the father would instruct his son more carefully, and the son would receive more attention from his father than from his teacher. This should not seem like some strange precedent. Cato the Censor[24] taught himself, and brought his son to great perfection, without the aid of any governor or teacher. Octavian Augustus[25], being emperor, had no qualms about teaching his two adopted sons. The iniquity of our time is such that men would consider it a monstrous thing to see a father, who is a gentleman, teach his children.

William. The shame is greater for those who, unable or unwilling to instruct their children themselves, do not care to entrust them to others.

Anniball. A man may see that they do not know the difference between the learned and ignorant, and the ignorant are worse than the dead in comparison to the learned.

William. However, the abuse is such that the wealthy of our time do not want their children to break their heads with study and do not want them to learn to read. I know many of them, rich in life but poor in culture, who enter the stores of merchants and pharmacies where their boys and apprentices write letters for their friends. Thus, they simultaneously betray both their secrets and ignorance. Oh, what a beautiful spectacle this is! I will never forget, not long ago in the office of an advocate, I heard one of his clerks (who had just written a letter for a gentleman present) ask him how he should address the letter, so he might put it in the heading. The gentleman responded that he did not need to write anything else but: *"To my gossip in Cremona"*. The clerk said that it was necessary to specify his name for the letter to reach the hands of his gossip. The man replied that his name was not important, because it was enough to say, *"To my gossip"* since everyone knew him.

Anniball. I want to believe he was a gentleman because you name him so, but in this doltish simplicity, he showed himself to be a clown, much like this one, when a physician asked him what country he was from, answered, *"You should be able to tell by my piss."* These rich folk without knowledge, or rather mindless bodies, are called sheep with golden fleeces by Diogenes. Therefore, they must take care to ensure their children learn. Just as the poor are driven to study by necessity, the rich are

Civil Conversation III

hindered by it through indulgence. They do not realize, except when it is too late, that learning is more necessary for them than for the poor, because they have more dealings in the world and need more ingenuity to preserve their riches, which, being brittle, fragile, and corruptible, can hardly last unless they are preserved with the sweet syrup of wisdom. A man will certainly live a better life with little obtained by virtue than with a great deal given by fortune. Those who take pride in the abundance of riches show that they do not know what happened to the gourd that boasted of having risen above the pine tree. Those who are wise, the richer they are, the better they will consider that riches are obtained by travel, preserved by fear, and lost by sorrow, and those who rely on them will be deceived. True riches are those that cannot be lost, once obtained. Therefore, discreet fathers will take care to educate their children in learning, persuading them that they are never rich until they are educated. Remember the example of Philip, king of Macedon, who as soon as his son Alexander was born, wrote letters to Aristotle, signifying the joy he felt, not so much at having a son, but because he was born in his time, to whose instruction and the government he had already entrusted. This prompts me, on this occasion, to be charitable to our generation, which holds little regard for the men who not only instruct us

Parents and children

in learning, but also in life, which are the two greatest goods that can be desired in this world. That is why they should not be despised but revered as much as our fathers.

Since many teachers are excellent in learning, but lewd in life, the father must be very cautious in his choice. What his son gains in one way, he loses in another, for he must take the same care to make him virtuous, as educated, and he should be more careful to make him good than to leave him possessions. Just as one said, "*If your son is wise and honest, you shall leave him enough goods; but if he is a fool, you shall leave him too many. For fools are not made to possess wealth.*" If the child is not fitted for learning, the father must not fail to employ him in other things, because there is nothing more dangerous than an idle young man. Just as the tree that does not blossom in the spring bears no fruit at the harvest, a child will never live honestly, as a man, who does not exercise himself virtuously while a child. Among other occasions of bad success for children, there is the one where the father, in time, is careless in helping them raise themselves from the ground.

William. What do you mean by that?

Anniball. The father, concerned about his son's progress, is often so curious to see him thoroughly instructed in worldly things, forgetting that the principle of wisdom is the fear of God; he does not care at all to instruct him in the Christian faith. Hence, this unhappy child, educated completely in worldly things and deprived of the true light, fails to see the right path and goes astray.

William. You hit the nail on the head. The wisdom of the world is foolishness before God. It is impossible to live well if you do not know God.

Anniball. This Christian admonition corresponds with what the divine Philosopher Plato said, when they cry out against their parents, who show themselves to be ignorant of what they ought to be doing, running up and down this and that road, devoting all their attention to amassing wealth and taking little care of the children who will possess it. They do not teach them either in the virtue of justice, or liberality, so they may distribute, use, and bestow their goods as they ought to do. In so doing, it can be said that they provide for the superfluous things and neglect the necessary ones. The Persians knew this very well, though ignorant of the true worship of God, were especially careful that their children should be instructed in justice and virtue.

Therefore, parents should take care of both the mind and the bodies of their children. Since the mind is better than everything else, it is right to devote our main care to it. Because the mind of

Parents and children

infants is like a pair of tables, where nothing is written on it, and like a tender twig that can be bent in any way, it is clear that virtue or vice can be easily planted in it. It is known that things that are learned when you are young are best preserved in memory. Fathers should instruct their children in the best things, that is, in the fear and love of God, holding as a general rule, *"He who knows everything and does not know God, knows nothing."*

William. If parents are unwilling or unable to be with their children all the time to keep them on the right path, they must provide them teachers, no less pious and learned, who every day, at the most opportune times, will teach them some devout prayers and instruct them in the fear of God. These teachers should always mingle with the ordinary lessons of some divine precepts. By imprinting in their tender hearts devotion and religion, for as long as they live, they will continue in godliness, and after death unite themselves with Christ.

Anniball. You say this well. If the father is diligent in instructing his children in God's law, he will be rewarded that his children will honor and respect him, knowing that it is a commandment of God that they should do so.

To the preceding occasion of poor success for children, we can add this; when the father sets before them a stained and gloomy glass to look at, that is when he sets a bad example for them. The Romans were very circumspect in this respect. Their modesty and discretion were so great that the father never let himself be seen in the company of his son like this. It was considered a serious fault of the father to let his son see him naked. No wonder Cato the Censor had Manlius expelled from the Senate, just for kissing his wife in the presence of his daughter. We can see that it is not enough for the father to appoint good masters over his children and to see them well-educated if above all he is not cautious in showing himself before them, as he wishes them to be. The master does not do them much good through his good instructions, as the father does them harm through his bad example. The children are more inclined to follow their father's footsteps than the precepts of the master. It is so natural that the son should resemble the father in gaming, swearing, and other vices. If by chance any son does not follow his father in these vices but lives virtuously and honestly, the world will find it hard to believe that he does so. Because of this negative opinion that has been conceived about the father, most believe that the child will be heir to his vices, as well as his lands. When they cannot find any fault in the son, some still do not refrain from striking him in the teeth, saying, "*He was the son of the worst man in the world.*" Likewise, if the

Parents and children

father is honest and the son lewd, the father's good name is questioned, and others think it impossible that the son could do wrong unless the father leads him awry.

It was thought that if some Roman gentlemen were too strict with their sons, they did not do it out of their displeasure for them, but out of the protection they had for their renown, and the desire to maintain their credit and reputation. I would, therefore, have the father live his life in a regular and orderly fashion, both for his own sake and the honor and benefit of his children. Seeing the virtue shine in their father's actions will motivate them to imitate him. Seeing those of the household quietly and reverently waiting on him, ready to execute his commands when he raises his finger, are shown an example of how to perform their duties and not be inferior in obedience to servants and strangers. Moreover, they should strive to resemble their father in actions, so they may receive in the future the same reverence from their servants as their father's servants have for him. The father who sets a bad example for his children will in time be despised by them and be forsaken by them, and do not provide assistance to him in his last days, or on his last day, the last duty to close his eyes. Besides, the father living disorderly and dishonestly often hoards those goods on which his children should live.

Civil Conversation III

William. That agrees with this saying,

> *The children cried often,*
> *for the faults of the father.*

Anniball. There are some cases in which infants, who have committed no offense, are punished for the guilt of their fathers. Thinking to myself that such a law is too rigorous, I asked Master Francesco Beccio one day what prompted Emperor Justinian to establish such a severe law. Among the many reasons he mentioned to me the principal one was that the father, naturally fearing the misfortune of his children more than his own, can restrain himself better from committing such offenses for which the children must bear the punishment. In this way, we know that the father's bad life brings his children loss and shame, and he should not be persuaded that it is enough to give good advice to his children unless his actions follow that advice. Children do not respect so much what the father says as what he does, as the crawfish sometimes did, who is told by his mother that it was very unseemly for him to go backward. As he did, he replied, *"Show me the right way, and you shall see I will follow you."*

He who wishes to amend his children must first reform himself by the example of piety, charity, justice, and the other virtues, make them charitable, just, and virtuous. When he has walked upright by himself, he may boldly correct others to stop, as Dionysius once did, when taking his son to task, said to him, *"Have you ever seen me commit such a fault?"* *"No"*, said the son, *"You have not had a king for your father."* To which he replied, *"Nor will you be a king for your son."* It came to pass, in the end, because of his cruelty and tyranny, he was driven out of his kingdom and was compelled by necessity to come and go until he found a way to teach children and start a school.

Let us turn our attention to the other occasions of unfortunate conversations between father and son. There are two that come to mind. One, when the father must be more than a mother, and the other, when he is more than a father.

William. What do you mean he must be more than a mother?

Anniball. When he is so blinded that he does not see his son's imperfections, or if he does see them, he is ready to praise or excuse them, so that if his son is haughty or harebrained, he calls him courageous. If he is contemptible and mean-spirited, he considers him modest. If he bloviates, he wants to make him, in the name of God, an orator. In flattering himself he creates, in his imagination, the best son in the world. With this blindness, fathers of only one son are mostly consoled.

Let me tell you a story about a young man about fifteen or sixteen years old, with a very sharp mind, but otherwise vicious, dissolute, and lewd, through the fault of his father and mother. They are so far from correcting him, that they dare not even threaten him, nor say any word to him that would displease him. I remember when he was five or six years old if anyone told them that they had to reprimand him for some fault he had committed, they excused him at once, saying he was not old enough to know he had done something wrong. When he was seven or eight, they would never beat or threaten him, doubting that through great fear and the disturbance of the spirits, his blood might be irritated and inflamed, which could cause him to develop a fever. When he was ten, they did not think it proper to disturb or molest him, alleging that whipping and threats might abate his courage and take away his noble stomach. Because, of all his horrible deeds, he is hated by the whole city. Yet, his parents still make excuses for him, saying, *"He must first grow up and then will become wise."* In a few days, they will send him to school, where he will learn. When he is old enough to be hanged at the gallows, I expect to hear him before the people lay the blame on his father and mother and justly curse their foolish love, their shameful arrogance, and their suffering, attempting, as he once did, to tear off their noses or ears with his teeth.

William. In this way, we can see that a child, with good intelligence, raised poorly, will prove to be bad. I wish you had said that in the end he beat his father to make amends, or drove him out of the house as the snake was driven out of the urchin. To give a child so much liberty is to put weapons in his hands, which he often uses against his parents. This overwhelming compassion is common to the mother, who usually brings up her children with more affection and discretion. There are few who, following the example of the Spartan women, have the heart to say to their children in giving them a target, *"Return with your shield or on it."*[26] Most strive to contrast every good thought that comes from their child with gestures and manners similar to women.

Anniball. It is difficult for a mother to be fond of her children and wise to them at the same time.

William. The right love is to beat and correct them when they deserve it, as the Poet says,

The rod does not make the mother's love less.

Civil Conversation III

Anniball. If an excess of love is reprehensible in the mother, it is much more so in the father. His job is to examine and correct the faults of his children. He can assure himself that the only way to spoil them is to be too affectionate and tender with them.

William. Who are these fathers you call more than fathers?

Anniball. Those who are too cruel to their children and continually beat them like slaves, for the slightest fault in the world.

William. In truth, these fathers are hated by all men, because without discretion they measure their children by themselves and require of them an impossible thing, which is to make them grow old in their youth, without allowing them to enjoy any of the liberty which is permitted at their age. In my opinion, they deserve no other name than that of a schoolmaster, because they cannot educate their children well unless they have the rod in their hands. If they were good fathers, they would be content that their children should learn from them, to know that all the guidance of human laws is nothing, but to refrain from being bad and to strive to be good and honest, which a child is brought up by love rather than by force. The authority that some ignorant fathers assume is so great that without regard to age, time, place, degree, fashion, or anything else, keep their children under control

Parents and children

by force and make them do anything contrary to their minds, even wearing clothes according to the fashions from the past.

Anniball. They are certainly doing wrong, making their children not love them. The children obey them from fear rather than from affection. Moreover, they do not consider that beating them without measure and keeping them in constant fear, is the reason why the children cannot determine the kind of life they are naturally inclined towards. It dulls their spirit and suppresses their natural vigor, so that there is no more metal in them, and always fear failure in their actions. They never succeed, and when around others do not know where to look or what to do. Therefore, they should cease to continue the horrible beatings, and consider their children cannot have the best understanding and experience in things, which helps them to be supported when they do wrong.

William. I like those fathers who know how to hold their children's respect, only by shaking their heads or making some other similar sign. They can correct them just by a word and make them ashamed of their mistakes. I am convinced that few fathers know how to keep their children in line. They are either too rough or too gentle with their children, where one drives them to despair; the other leads them to dissolution.

Civil Conversation III

Anniball. You have to think that the child has been given a father and a mother so that the wisdom of the one and the love of the other, develop meaning in their life. Therefore, the severity of the father is somewhat mitigated by the leniency of the mother.

William. In my opinion, you can add one more thing to the disagreements between a father and child, which is the father's partial love for them.

Anniball. Do you believe that to be a fault?

William. Does it seem reasonable to you that he embraces and loves one more than another? Being that they are of his flesh and blood, he has a cheerful countenance for some of them and a stern look for others.

Anniball. Of all the sonnets and other compositions you have made, do you prefer some to others? And perhaps which ones are better or worse? Are you certain that your father does not love all of his children equally, yet the ones that he loves least cannot rightly complain about him?

William. I do not give my father any opportunity to use me worse than the others, and if he did, I would have reason to complain about him as long as I am alive.

Anniball. You have a reason if he mistreats you, but not if he loves you less than another.

Parents and children

Inequality of love is permitted by the father, but not mistreatment.

William. What do you mean by that?

Anniball. A merchant father has a scholar, soldier, and merchant for sons. Of these three, he is most likely to love the merchant more, because he sees him as similar to himself in life and manners. His other two sons will have to put up with him because by nature we are inclined to like the things that resemble ourselves. They will have a reason to complain about him as being unjust if he does not give them an allowance for diet, clothing, and other necessities equal to what he does the merchant son.

William. Oh! How difficult is it for the father, once this lack of affection has entered his heart, to administer fairness with such indifference?

Anniball. The greater the wisdom of the father when he prefers the merits of his children to his own partial affection, makes his senses yield to reason and shows himself equal to all in his actions. I do not deny that the father, by his authority, should distribute his favors as he sees fit, to one more, to another less, according to the behavior and actions of his children. Through gentle usage, he encourages one who is well-behaved to do well, and harsh punishment leads an unruly child to goodness. If he has a child that has lost his grace, with no hope of recovery, he may legitimately not only love them less than others but also cast them out of his favor, as Aristippus[27] did with one of his lewd sons. When he was rebuked by one of his friends, who urged him to consider that his son was a piece of his own flesh and came from his loins, he replied, *"Lice and many other superfluous things come from a man's body, and being diseased, they must be cast away."*

Those fathers should be reproached who, with unjust partiality and without any reasonable consideration, regard one son as legitimate and the other as a bastard. It follows that the one who is so grossly disregarded not only fails in his affection for his father but also begins to enter into a secret war with his other brother. In this way the father, whose chief duty is to establish peace and harmony among his children, through his indiscreet and unjust partiality plants among them a root of continual discord. Therefore, a father should be well advised on how to willingly prefer one son over the other, and not to do so on every occasion. Some will do so, not because of any fault in them, but because of some natural defect. In my judgment, they do great harm by making their innocent child bear the punishment of their imperfections, which at the time they cause it, were in no doubt affected by some infirmity of the mind or body.

Parents and children

William. I cannot stand the folly of some fathers who make one of their children their most cherished minion when they have no good qualities in them and are not ashamed to let everyone know their affection and love without cause.

Anniball. Take the example of the ape that had two little ones in her litter, she loved one but did not care for the other. On one occasion she was driven to flee from her den. She picked up the one she loved in her arms and placed the other on her back. While running, she tripped which caused her to fall and be driven into the ground, killing the one in her arms that she loved so well while the one on her back suffered no harm. In this way, we can see that the father often does penance for his offense of doting and affection. Most of the time the children whom we fuss about the most, fall the worst. It often happens that the children on the right side, as a result of their wanton and delicate education, turn out to be dolts, fools, and simple sots. While, on the contrary, those who come in through the back door, driven out of their father's house and forced to move out on their own, often, by their own efforts and labor, come to be better off than their father and their brothers, whom they often help and assist in their difficulties.

William. Therefore, we can boldly say that the father's injustice generates disagreement between his children and him, regardless of the unequal love I have proposed.

Anniball. Yes, but if we talked about a merchant, the father of a doctor and scholar, another occasion comes to my mind, giving rise to quarrels between father and child, that is, when the father is inferior in the vocation to the son. For instance, if the father is an ignorant man or a simple country fellow, and the son is a learned or a brave courtier, you will have much difficulty in making these two agree. The father, according to his nature and calling, deals with low and base things and does not know or value the high standards of his son. Though he says nothing, he is unhappy in his mind, to see his son maintain a serious-mindedness commensurate with his wealth, and be so lavish in his diet and dress. He would rather see him convert his earnings into the land, cattle, or some other commodity.

There are others, who are not so foolish. They know the worth of their children and what belongs to their estate. Yet, because they are inferior to them grieve in their heart so that they always endeavor to resist both in word and deed their position in society.

On the other hand, you will see the son. Either because he sees his father not taking account of him as others do or because he sees him leading a hard life and never wanting to get out of the

Parents and children

mire. Withdrawing his affection from him, never wanting him to come and see him, thinking he dishonors him. If he is not wicked enough to wish him dead he is at least satisfied, when he sees him, for some illness or infirmity lying in some corner of the house.

William. To this end, I heard the other day of a wretched man who was so unhappy that he would never allow his son, who was a doctor, to have a man serve him. When his son went out, he used a poor man who lived nearby to follow him instead of a servant. One morning while the son was waiting for the neighbor at the door to accompany him to mass, being very late, the father, thinking of his own misery and seeing that his son was scantily clad, put on his cloak, and said to him, *"Go to mass, and I will follow you,"* thinking that his son was such a fool to accept his offer and show himself in such a shameful way.

Anniball. I think he offered to serve his son because he did not want to give his poor neighbor dinner, rather than out of shame for his own misery or respect for his son's honesty.

William. Now that we have come across this example, I would like to know from you, in this difference of degree and vocation, who should come first, the father or the son?

Anniball. Taurus[28], the philosopher, has already

Civil Conversation III

decided this doubt after a visit by a Roman president and his father. Having only one chair available while another was being brought in, asked the father to sit down. The father replied that his son should sit first since he was the president. For all that, he requested him to sit down still and that afterward he would explain which of the two should have the advantage. Once the father and the son were seated, he pronounced, *"In public places and affairs, the father, being a private person, must give way to the son, who is appointed in office, as the one who represents the majesty of the prince, or the commonwealth. Otherwise, in private places, assemblies, and meetings with friends, the public authority must give way to the father's jurisdiction."*

William. The father of the doctor we are talking about should have had his son follow him that morning on his way to mass in his long gown, since he was practicing no profession but only that of a doctor. This would have been quite a sight and would have made everyone laugh, even though there was no reason to.

Anniball. If one had to laugh at it, one would also marvel at the example of Sempronius Gracchus, consul of Rome, while maintaining his state in public and meeting with his father Quintus Fabius Maximus, the proconsul, ordered his sergeants to command his father to dismount from his horse. The father promptly dismounted, recognizing the position of his son, because he knew how to maintain the majesty of the Roman Empire. Now, to return to our subject, there is still an occasion for disagreement between the father and the child, and that is when the father does not want his children to grow up.

William. What do you mean by that?

Anniball. When the authority of old age, ambition, greed, or excessive belief in his own sufficiency make the father want to maintain his paternal authority. Although his children have reached adulthood and are perfectly fulfilled in every sense, he does not allow them to live their life or have any more freedom than they had when they were children.

William. I think they have good reason to be discontented, knowing themselves to be sufficient men, and thus being taken by all, are nevertheless used by their father as children. Therefore, I cannot blame them much, if instead of loving him, they wish for his death by delaying the execution of the sentence pronounced against him so long ago. In this regard, I know a gentleman who has lived forty years under a wealthy father and is so miserable that it causes despair in him. He often tells his companions that he is a fool to live so long and that it is high time for him to go to another world; adding that his life will be of no use to him when it falls into his hands, by the course of nature, when he will be forced to take care of the old man.

Anniball. A certain country fellow used to say that through his labor, he obtained five loaves of bread every day. When asked how he distributed them, he replied, "*I keep one for myself, throw away another, another I pay for at home, and the other two I lend out.*" When asked to explain his riddle, he would say, "*I take one for myself, another I take back to give to my stepmother, give one to my father, and lend two to my children.*" By this example, which is nobler than lacking in social graces, children should learn to love and be grateful to their fathers and fathers to be liberal to their children, remembering that, in their old age and necessity, what they have lent to their children will be returned by their children. Therefore, the fathers whom we have just spoken about do not take this into account, and it may be said that they have become doting old men, much like a child who has no judgment.

William. If this is due to age, I will not say, but these men were worthy to dwell among the Caspians[29] who, when their father reached seventy, immediately killed him and fed him to the beasts. I will say that they should recognize their insufficiency and lack of judgment and defer the order of home and life to their children,

Parents and children

who have the discretion to deal with such important matters. If the cause is covetousness, they should consider that it is a shameful thing in old folk, of all people. There is nothing more absurd or devoid of reason than for a man to make large provisions for his journey when he is almost at the end of his journey. If they have accumulated their wealth for themselves, some of it will serve as their support, but if they have worked for their children, it is right that they should leave it to them, as soon as they have the discretion to know how to use it. If ambition is to blame, the poor souls should take an example from princes and rulers who, seeing their children fit to rule the people, willingly give up their possessions, kingdoms, and empires to them, for which we have many examples. Should they think too highly of themselves, let them learn to know that children today are born wise. Since men do not live as long as they did in the past, they reach perfection sooner than they did in the past.

Anniball. It is difficult for these old men to profit from these good admonitions, because their vices, through time, have taken root in them too deep to be uprooted. Nevertheless, we will not cease to advise the father, if he wants the happiness and advancement of his son, to discreetly allow him some freedom in the affairs of the house, allowing him sometimes to invite,

Civil Conversation III

welcome, treat his companions with respect, entertain strangers, and, on occasion, use the goods of the house for his service. Above all, he should by example and admonition prevent covetousness and insatiable desire from entering his heart. This makes men wicked and unjust or at least does not allow them to live in peace and tranquility. In particular, the father, who is a gentleman, should have in mind that king who on entering his son's quarters and seeing there many pieces of the plate which he had given him said, *"I can see that you have no princely spirit, in you, seeing that of the many things I have given you, you have never made a friend."* That father should encourage his son to do liberal and chivalrous deeds. He should marry so, from time to time, if he has no other resources, he may learn to play the part of a good husband and to take care of the things of the house, which will enable him to preserve and increase his property to guard against falling into decay. This will result in at least three good effects.

The first is the love of the son who, seeing his father withdraw little by little from the government of the house, retreats to his room receiving a marvelous contentment from it. He believes in his mind that he is bound to him, and not only honors him but also wishes that he will live a long time.

The second is the welfare of the son who in this

way, after the death of his father, will not need to seek advice and help from his friends and relatives, nor to rely on the discretion of his servants for the order of his house, thanks to the goodness and foresight of his father everything has been managed by him for a long time.

The third is the sweet repose and contentment that the father enjoys in old age, both because he feels free from all encumbrances and annoyances and because he sees his son, by his example, govern his house orderly. For my part, I think it is the greatest happiness in the world for a man to have around him many good children, brought up to perfection, whom he may well call the light of his eyes and the staff of his age. I am not surprised that the very prudent lady Cornelia showed her neighbor, when asked to see her chains and jewels, her learned and virtuous children. I think it must be a great comfort to the father to see proof that his son discreetly knows how to dispose of his property and manage his house than do it himself. Now, when the father has arrived at the haven of this happiness and consolation, it seems to me that he can look forward with joy to the last hours of his life, and fall asleep with the greatest contentment.

William. It is far better to give way to one's children of one's own accord than to stay as long as they have to, despite their teeth. Ptolemy[30]

Civil Conversation III

gave the kingdom of Egypt to his son and said that there was nothing more honorable and acceptable than to be the father of a king, which above all of his other acts increased the immortal glory of Charles V.[31]

Anniball. Although it is written in the scriptures, *"Never, as long as you live, give anyone power over you — whether son, wife, brother, or friend. Don't give your property to anyone; you might change your mind and have to ask for it back."*[32] Yet there have been in the past, and there are still today, many wise fathers who leave their sons both authority and their property, without incurring any inconvenience, because they do so in such a way that they do not submit to them, and cannot live without them. As for the inheritance that is rightfully the child's, when he sees the father keeping it entirely for himself, he not only desires to obtain it but seeks to recover it as if it were his due. When he is compelled to wait for it until his father's death, he realizes that he got it from his hand at his death, and not from his father's hand, and never has the opportunity to thank him for it.

William. All the occasions that you have stated so far, between the disagreement of the father and the children, come from the fault of the father. It would be good to see what occasions come from the responsibility of the children.

Anniball. When the father acts in such a way

that none of the occasions we have spoken of on his part have occurred, I think the child will have no reason to disagree with him. Therefore, this saying applies, "*The son is for the most part like the father and the daughter ordinarily follows in the mother's footsteps.*" Since some children are untoward enough through no fault of the father, I think we can briefly point out to the child a form of conversation with the father, so there is no occasion for trouble or disagreement on their part.

Responsibilities of the father

***W**illiam.* Although through our discourse, I have learned in part how the father should conduct himself towards the child, I would like you to briefly gather the main points concerning the father, and then move on to the duties of the son, as you have just offered to do.

Anniball. I will do so. First of all, I will make it clear to the father that there is nothing in the world in which more care and diligence should be given than to the education and instruction of the children. This alone, for the most part, insures the maintenance or decay of the home. He starts by providing their tender minds with the fear and knowledge of God, righteousness, and truth, as well as virtue and good conditions, so they learn to live as if they were about to die.

He should endeavor to keep them obedient, by

Responsibilities of the father

love rather than fear, and to help them to do well, by their own accord, than by the imposition of others. It is unseemly for one that is free to live in bondage, nor is fear a good guardian of virtue.

In teaching them, he prefers to play with them, rather than terrify them, because no art or discipline sticks in the mind when it is forcibly driven into it. No matter how advanced they may be, he does not stop encouraging and urging them forward, knowing that no horse does not need spurring. He does not let them be idle but teaches them to be accustomed to working, so they can bear labor, as Milo[33] was able to carry a bull because he used to carry a calf.

He should not get angry with his children. A good father uses wisdom instead of anger and issues a small punishment for a great fault, yet is not so foolish and pitiful to forgive it. Knowing that by sparing the rod he may seem to hate his child, using it a lot may diminish their courage and make them dull and desperate.

He needs to provide them with good teachers and governors who will continually assist them. Young children must be supported like young trees; otherwise, the tempest of vices could break or bend them crooked. He should not allow them to spend time in the company of servants and the lower class, because they will encounter corrupt words and vile conditions, which they will never forget. He needs to take care to identify in their childhood the kind of life they are naturally inclined towards, to guide them diligently toward it, for an adverse beginning always has an unfortunate end.

They should be taught to govern themselves with the bridle and the spur, that is, with shame in dishonest things and a desire for glory in good things. Without just cause, he does not use partiality among his children, unless he wants them to quarrel with each other.

In all his actions he should show himself to be serious and modest. By doing well himself, he sets an example for his children to do the same, remembering how shameful it is to defile oneself by vice, which others should take as an example of virtue. In his old age, when his children are grown, he does not deny them, through covetousness, reasonable allowances for living. He should treat them in such a way that they may think they enjoy his estate, no less in his lifetime, than in death. Otherwise, instead of honoring him, they will desire to have him buried.

Lastly, let him be so attentive to his children, that when he dies, he will not feel his conscience burdened by having to account for his neglect of them. Persuading himself that among all the abuses of the world (recited by an excellent

Responsibilities of the father

author in this class, "*A wise man without works, an old man without religion, a young man without obedience, a rich man without charity, a woman without honesty, a master without virtue, a contentious Christian, a proud poor man, an unjust King*") there is nothing worse than a negligent father. Therefore, if nature compels him, guided by his conscience, and bound by honor and honesty to take care of his children, let him in no way abandon this care, but follow the example of good Aeneas[34], whose son Ascanius[35] was his only care.

Behavior of the child

William. For your convenience, I would like to briefly understand the duty of the child.

Anniball. If the child would consider the great and extreme love of his father for him, there would be no need to prescribe a form of conversation, for this consideration would be enough to keep him in his duty, and make him conform to his father's will and pleasure in all things. I could give many examples of pitiful fathers who, by some misfortune that befell their children, manifested their excessive love by voluntary death or some other painful effect. Let us consider the grief of King David,[36] who at the death of his son Absalom[37] was overcome by his affections (which in all other accidents he would dominate) that shedding tears so abundantly for the grief he felt, was led to burst out in these

Behavior of the child

complaints, *"My son Absalom, my son Absalom, who will let me die for you."* He was so grieved by the death of his son, even though his son had already killed his other son Amnon[38] and had done him a thousand insults, and had finally conspired against him and his kingdom.

Since children have no regard for this tender love of their parents as they ought to have, doing as you would have me do, they should know that the first law of nature is to honor their father and mother. The Spartans were accustomed to respecting their elders. Being accustomed to this reverence with those they have nothing to do with, they should have more honor and respect for their parents. If the Heathen observed the law so inviolably, all the more should the Christians observe it, who have received it from the very mouth of God who gives his blessing and promises the reward of long life to those who honor their father and mother.

No child should be so devoid of grace and reverence, among countless others, as to forget these three benefits received from the father, namely his being, nurture, and instruction. Each of these is sufficient to persuade them that after God there is nothing more to be honored than the father and mother.

If their father is unkind and malicious toward them, the many benefits they receive from him counterbalance this cruelty and urge them to fulfill their duty, following the example of the young man who, when it was held against him that his father spoke ill of him, replied that he would not do so if he had no reason. Let them beware of harassing their parents in any way or contending with them, but overcome them with patience. They will never find a better friend than their father. They should always bear in mind that he who obstinately quarrels with his father provokes the wrath of God against him, so he will not pass his life quietly, nor come to his end honestly. Let them behave in such a way that their fathers have no reason to curse them and wish them ill, as Oedipus[39] did to his children, for God certainly hears the father's prayers against his children.

Do not let them think that they can demand, by any action or service, their father's kindness to them, nor fear to be found flatterers, by any praise they may give him, or by any kindness they may show him. When they have done their duty to the fullest they will not have done all that they should. Finally, let them support their parents in all difficulties and adversity, assuring them that those who abandon their parents will be forsaken by God, which is the greatest fault that can be committed.

William. From your pious admonitions it can be inferred that you cannot blame the wise Solomon, when asked why he did not make a

Behavior of the child

law against the murderers of their parents, he replied, *"No one, however wicked, would ever commit such monstrous impiety."* Do you have anything else to say about the conversation between the father and the son?

Anniball. Nothing else, except that his children do the same to him as he does to his father. There once was a father, who was driven out of his own house by his son and compelled to lodge in the spittle house.[40] Seeing his son pass by the door one day, begged him out of charity to at least send him a pair of sheets to lie on. The son, moved by his father's request, had no sooner returned home than he ordered one of his sons to carry a pair of sheets to the hospital for his grandfather. The child delivered only one, for which his father rebuked him on his return, and he replied, *"I will keep the other for you, when, in your old age, you go to the hospital, as my grandfather does now."* Thus, we will learn that our children will treat us as we treat our parents. This will serve to close our discourse on this conversation.

A little bit about daughters

William. I find your discourse perfect. If you please, could you make special mention of the daughters, because the father must behave differently towards them than towards his sons?

Anniball. I am afraid I cannot satisfy you on this point because nowadays the manner of bringing them up is so different, not only from country to country but from counties and cities. One cannot make a definitive rule for it. Some parents will not allow their daughters to set foot outside the house except once or twice a year and on certain solemn holidays. Others not only will enable them to keep company with their friends and relatives at home, but also to visit their friends abroad, and be present at banquets and meetings of friends. Some will teach them to write, read, and be proficient in poetry, music, and painting.

A little bit about daughters

Others only want them to learn the spinning of the distaff[41] and the house's administration. Does it seem possible to you to establish a set of rules that is compatible with all these diversities?

William. I remember reading of a very wise painter who, having to draw the singular beauty of Helen assembled a company of the most beautiful women he could find. Taking from each of them the part that was most excellent in them and reducing all their beauty into the form of Helen. I would like it if you could take those fashions and draw from each of these customs, from your best judgment, the parts that you like the best, to compile the form and manners of a perfect virgin.

Anniball. I would rather you convince me to run away than follow the painter's example. While he drew Helen, I think I would do better to represent Lucretia[42] or Virginia.[43]

William. You have surprised me, but I would like you to answer according to the simple meaning of my words.

Anniball. Even if I do, I must not follow the painter, because his painting tended only to one end, while fathers do not do so in the education of their daughters. Each of these diversities is commendable if properly understood.

William. I do not see how these extremes can be

commendable. Not allowing a young girl to go out once or twice a year and keeping her locked up like a holy relic, is the way to make her foolish, fearful, out of sorts in the company of others, and easier to catch in a net. If she is not accustomed to seeing the sun, as soon as she sets foot outside the house, her eyes are dazzled by the slightest of its rays and she falls backward. Now the other, who goes out every day with her mother and attends feasts and banquets, melt like wax in the fire. This gradually removes the modesty from her looks and gestures, appears in her behavior licentious and lascivious, so that she is taken for a mother rather than for a young girl. If there is nothing worse, the mother should at least be sure of this, as some folks are pressed by poverty and need to take movable goods from their house to the public square and sell them for less than they are worth, the mother who often takes her daughter to public places makes her less valued and worse off than she might otherwise be. I say nothing of those who are educated in their rooms to read, sing, compose verses, and never go down to the kitchen. I will leave that to the poor husbands, whose house goes to ruin, and often their honor as well, just to have an educated wife. If you look at one of those who can do nothing but spin and sow, you will see in her attire, speech, and behavior the very figure of a country milkmaid, who will have as much grace among other

A little bit about daughters

women as a satyr would have among the nymphs. That is why I think it would be fitting that you take the best part of each and make a perfect one, according to your fancy.

Anniball. I will do so in a few words, answering that all these different ways are commendable, when they tend to a commendable end. It is therefore fitting those discreet fathers, who entrust their daughters, should first measure their degree and disposition, and then position them accordingly. If they deem them fit to enter religion, the mother, who should have the chief responsibility for them, should endeavor to divert them from all worldly vanities and educate them to such sincerity of thought and purity of life. The vow they will make is beyond the possibilities of nature, and contrary to the liberty granted to mankind, will not be broken as is the case every day, and that this field shall not be polluted by prostitution and other filthiness, as it has been by Rhea[44], that Roman vestal, and various other Roman votaries, since her time. If they intend to give them in marriage, the father must consider what vocation and nation his son-in-law will be from and then frame his daughter accordingly. If he intends to marry her into a country where women are bound to a strict life, and cooped up by their husbands like hawks, lest they should yield to some prey they should not. It behooves the father to take away all liberty from her, keeping her inside, and accustom her to such a harsh and solitary life that it will not seem strange or painful to her when her husband forces her to do the same. On the contrary, if she marries in a freer country, such as Piedmont or our Montserrat, her father should loosen the reins a little and give her more freedom, so that she may adapt to the life that wives in that country lead and not be taken for a fool and a clown.

William. The father does not always have his son-in-law up his sleeve; marriages, as they say, are made in heaven and guided by fate. A father may be engaged in a matter for ten years and at a moment's notice be driven to change.

Anniball. I thought I said as much. Therefore, I think the father, not being certain of the marriage, should in this doubt carry a heavy, rather than a light, hand on the bridle. It is much easier to let the reigns loose afterward than to gather them up, once they have fallen on their neck.

William. Since you have fallen on this point of restraining liberty, I cannot refrain from talking about the abuse in this city, where a man sees nothing all day but women in the streets going from house to house, visiting some out of courtesy, and others (who have visited them before) out of duty, without any occasion. It is not because of a marriage or the death of some

A little bit about daughters

friend, but (as I have heard) if someone has only had a fever or has stayed in their room for a few days, all the women in the city run there in a row, as if it were a procession.

Anniball. The chances of these visits are so frequent and numerous that they devote six days a week to them. So much so that you will hear some of them complain that they hardly have any time on Saturdays to wash their hair. I will tell you that they are worthy of excuse, yes, and of praise if they do it out of charity, and not to show themselves in all their prowess, and to run up and down from place to place, to denounce and jeer at the faults of other homes. It is certain that the ladies of Mantua who are in this city mock or at least marvel at this fashion, so as not to give the impression of being ill-mannered, do nothing but run and trot up and down, conforming to the customs of our country's women.

William. If this custom were permitted, it would be good for the good of all, to introduce another, that while the wives go around gossiping, the husbands remain at home sewing and spinning, and attending to other things of the house, in their absence.

Anniball. I think it is well to let the wives go about as they please, and we should go home to the daughters, whom it is necessary to instruct in the things necessary to win the favor of their mistress. If their father intends to put them at court in the service of some princess, it behooves them to learn to read, write, speak, sing, play instruments, dance, and be able to do all that is incumbent of a courtier. Just like this Venetian Lady could do, who was praised because she knew how to use a book instead of wool, a pen instead of a spindle, and compose a poem instead of sowing seeds, things that nowadays happen to very few women, but in the past were common to many. I am sure I have seen the role of more than a thousand, who have excelled in divinity, philosophy, physics, music, painting, and all the sciences.

William. I have seen some petty gentlewomen around the Queen of France, who have obtained such credit, only by some of those good parts you recite. They marry the principal gentlemen of France, without their father giving them a penny in dowry. A private gentleman has no need in his house for singing or dancing.

Anniball. You said it well. If the father does not want to bestow his daughter on some man of great vocation, he should have her practice spinning the wheel rather than playing instruments.

William. What about the daughters not only of gentlemen but also of merchants and artisans learning to read and write?

Anniball. Since these things are at least

A little bit about daughters

convenient, if not entirely necessary, I do not dislike them, as long as they are well-used.

William. I would think you are right if the women of Italy followed the trials in law and frequented the houses of the judges and lawyers so they could be acquainting themselves with their affairs, or if in commerce, they kept the books as several women in France do. By teaching our women to read and write, we only allow them to peruse Boccaccio's[45] hundred novellas and to write amorous and lascivious letters.

Anniball. We also give them the ability to read about the lives of the saints, keep the household accounts, and write their thoughts to their absent husbands without revealing their secrets to any secretary. Moreover, you can be assured that those women who cannot write, nor write love letters will do so, if they are willing with words, yes, and if their voice were to fail them, they would do it with signs.

To end this subject, I conclude with respect for daughters, that in such diversities that are used nowadays for their education, I cannot give a more suitable announcement than the following, *"Fathers should give all their study and industry to bring them up chaste, both in body and mind, for a man cares little for immaculate flesh, if the thought is defiled."* Therefore, it is necessary to put into their hearts a godly imagination, so that from

Civil Conversation III

their inner purity the bright rays of modesty may shine outwardly on their face and countenance. Since beauty is a fragile and dangerous thing, those who are beautiful are all the more in need of this virtue, to keep their beauty intact, for beauty in an unchaste woman serves no more purpose than a gold ring in a pig's snout and, to make a long story short, they must understand that, as a Poet once said,

A woman devoid of honesty
cannot boast of being beautiful.

Differences between sons and daughters

***W**illiam.* Before moving on to the conversation between brothers, I would like you to establish the difference that must exist between sons and daughters in conversation.

Anniball. I do not know if, while flipping through your books, you have lingered on that point where Cicero gives his daughter and son-in-law a nip, both at the same time.

William. I do not know if I have read it, and if I did, I have forgotten it.

Anniball. His Son-in-law was so delicate that he walked to the door with a slow, shuffling step, like a woman. His daughter, on the other hand, walked with great strides like a man. Her father, seeing this, said to her cheerfully, *"Daughter, go as your husband does."*; which must be understood, not only of the comings and goings, but of all other actions, where it is indecent for a woman to resemble a man, or a man a woman. Therefore, a maiden should conduct herself in such a way that, above all, she shows inwardly and outwardly the youthful modesty which is proper to maidens. It is a monstrous and naughty thing, to see a maiden use so much liberty and boldness in her gestures, looks, and words, as is proper to men. Let the maidens learn in all their behavior to express that modesty, which is so proper to their well-being, making sure that though they are provided with all the other beauties, graces, and virtues of the world, if this bright sun does not shine in them, all the other stars that borrow its light will have no effect. Just as goldsmiths sometimes cover their objects and jewelry with glass to make them stand out better; a maiden, under the veil of modesty, must enclose all her other perfections to increase their brightness and more strongly attract the eyes and hearts of others, to hold her in admiration.

On the other hand, it is the worst spectacle there can be to see sons who, by their gestures and appearance as women, make men doubt whether they are male or female. I will repeat that the father misunderstands, with too much strictness he makes his son as fearful as a rabbit. Whereby, when the young man comes before his

Differences between sons and daughters

superiors, he shows that he has no tongue in his mouth, or speaks and answers so foolishly, that he is laughed at. Therefore, he does not willingly seek any company, but hides, just like the following saying,

He hides in the thickets, like a deer pursued by dogs.

A Deer Attacked by Dogs, Jean-Baptiste Oudry (1686 - 1755), 1725.

Civil Conversation III

William. In my opinion, the French use great discretion in this regard. From infancy, they encourage their children to talk to their superiors. This way they learn to be bold and resolute in their behavior, and they are not embarrassed in the presence of the king, or amongst their peers.

Anniball. That boldness is not found in many Italians. I have known many excellent and worthy men who, coming before princes, have been so astonished and fearful that their complexion changed, sweat ran down their faces, their voices trembled, their bodies shook, and their words came out so foolishly, that they clearly showed what a troublesome situation they were in. Although wise men like it, and regard it as a sign of good nature, they show them the greatest affection. Such disturbances often hinder a man and are mocked as men who are not up to the mark. From this, we can infer the great wrong that fathers, mothers, and nurses do to young children when they amuse themselves by frightening their children with stories of Robin Hood and the like, thus offending God and making their children fearful and wicked. It is incumbent upon us, to make our children bold, and to teach them from the beginning to resist what frightens them, or else this proverb will be true to them, "*The wolf is cruel to the gentle dog.*" Therefore, we should take an example from the fox, who at first sight of the lion was anxious with fear, but seeing him again began to fear him only a little, and finally went to meet him with great courage. Thus, we can conclude that boldness is good in all things, and nothing is well done with doubt and fear.

William. If ever there was a time to put on a good face and be bold, it is undoubtedly now. This great reverence and modesty in action are considered more proper for men of the church than for courtiers, and although it is acceptable to those toward whom it is used, as you say, it is detrimental to those who will use it. While on the contrary, those who are bold in the company of others (provided they are discreet) are more esteemed and make a place for themselves everywhere, so neither the precepts of Cato nor the rules of the philosophers hold us in greater respect today than you say.

Anniball. I will not say that we should despise them, but I will say that as far as manners and behavior are concerned (as long as they are not contrary to honesty) we should adapt ourselves to the fashion of the countries and times in which we live. We should respond to the observers of antiquity as was done to Politian[46], who, meeting one of his friends who was going at a fast pace in the street, stopped him by the flap of his cloak, advising him to go more slowly, for Aristotle says, "*A slow pace is a sign of gravity*", who, stopping and looking him in the face, replied, *"I marvel at you, if Aristotle had only half the business I have, he would still be running, yet he would not have completed a third of it."*

To conclude, we will say that since men should not be Sardanapalus[47] or women Amazons, the father's task is to make sure that between his son and daughter, there is a difference in conversation, he in boldness, and she in modesty.

William. Now I think it would be appropriate for you to prescribe a form of conversation for widows.

Anniball. If we bring widows into society, what kind of widows will they be? We can propose to them either the conversation of a second husband or a solitary life suitable for widows. If we have anything to say on the subject let us resolve ourselves by showing that the fate of widows is, of all others, the most unfortunate. Not only those who live licentiously, but even the wisest and the most honest, serve as targets for evil tongues, and it seems that the more they cover their faces and eyes with their masks, the more men are quick to discover some fault in them. Therefore, if they wish to avoid such harm, they must be careful (especially the young) in speech, appearance, dress, and behavior not to give the slightest suspicion of vanity that there may be. If a reasonable occasion does not compel them, they must not

Differences between sons and daughters

keep any company but keep themselves honest in name and action. They should above all things banish idleness and ease, and apply themselves continually to some commendable exercise, remembering this saying, *"But she who gives herself to pleasure is dead while she is living."*[48] They should remember the example of the renowned widow Judith,[49] who because of her great riches, youth, and singular beauty was persuaded to marry again. She was content to be a widow to marriage, woolen garments to sumptuous apparel, abstinence to gluttony, watchfulness to sleep, prayer to loitering. Armed with these weapons, she cut off the head of Holofernes,[50] that is, of the devil.

Brothers

William. According to the order of our conversation, can we discuss the conversation between brothers now?

Anniball. Of course, I will expressly speak of what is necessarily implied in what I have already said. If the father uses such care in the education of his children, and the children diligently follow the instructions of the father as we have counseled them, it should be possible for the brothers to live in unity and friendship, and govern themselves together with one mind and accord. Therefore, we need not say much about it.

William. If you consider the rarity of agreements and the frequent arguments between siblings, you will want to have something to talk about, if you don't have time to talk.

Brothers

Anniball. Just as the physician is concerned with discovering the cause of the disease, and once he has found it, does not delay in finding a remedy to cure it. So, according to our custom, we must first have recourse to the causes which give rise to this discord between brothers and, once known, quickly find a remedy to cure it.

William. We must look for the causes because the effects are so horrible and wonderful. In my opinion, the rage of wild beasts is not as great as the hatred and resentment of brothers who live in discord.

Anniball. To prove your point, it is said that the animosity between Eteocles and Polynices[51] was so great that their bodies were burned together and the flames miraculously saw them separate from each other. This clearly shows that death was unable to settle their disputes or end their cancerous hatred.

William. I knew two Italian brothers in France of great courage and prowess. Both men-at-arms and working for the king. On one small occasion, they quarreled with each other to such an extent that they stopped sleeping in the same quarters, as they had done for the past ten years. They also ceased to talk with one another and salute each other. Their hatred had festered in their hearts so much that if anyone, of goodwill, went to befriend them, dealing with one and sometimes the other, they got nothing out of it but their ill will. At that same time Count Hercole Strozzi, ambassador of Mantua, had a house in Paris where, to maintain his rank and generous nature, he entertained gentlemen of all countries. He was especially visited by Italian men-at-arms, who were sometimes seen at his table in numbers of ten so that he seemed to be their captain. Often one or the other of those brothers would stay with him. As Easter approached the Count thought that in these days of penance he could convince them to confess their faults, reconcile with each other, and live together as brothers again.

Count Hercole Strozzi (1473-1508)

He began by testing the younger brother's mind and resolve, trying to help him understand that he should humble himself to his elder brother, but he found his heart so hardened that he would not yield at all. He then addressed the other and endeavored, in many different ways, to get him to understand that it was his duty, as the elder and discreet one, to make up for his brother's shortcomings. This was so misinterpreted by the older brother that he told the Count that he half understood what he meant, and he was content to abstain from inhabiting his house so that those who were more in his favor might have free access to it. In short, all his attempts were in vain, as if they had been made against an invincible fortress. The best arrangement he could get from him was that he was content, concerning him, to be friendly with his brother in his presence, but would kill him afterward if he could. He never did do this, because a few days later, in that bad state of mind was killed at the battle of Saint-Quinten.[52]

Anniball. He thought he was showing the Count some courtesy by deferring his brother's death. It truly is a desperate remedy to put out the fire of discord, when it is already kindled in the hearts of two brothers. This makes me reflect on how it is possible to deal with something so far removed from all reason.

Civil Conversation III

William. Indeed it seems reasonable that a man is most offended by those who should not even offend him.

Anniball. It seems reasonable to me, that a man should be less offended by those who should hold him accountable.

William. Don't you know that where there is great love, there arises great hatred?

Anniball. Don't you know that where there is great love, there must also be great patience?

William. Yet, from my experience, you see the opposite.

Anniball. Brothers are often at odds because they have never agreed, but when they have lived together in love since childhood will endure any hurt or displeasure rather than fight with each other.

William. You mean the reason why brothers grow apart is due to a lack of love.

Anniball. If I were to say that, for this reason, I would be considered as foolish as the man who was asked why the dog followed his master, and answered, "*His master preceded him.*" You might also say, according to the proverb, "*I tried to fill your mouth with an empty spoon*", that is, to appear to teach and not teach. Therefore, if you want me to come to the correct conclusion about this discord, I will tell you that I have noticed the two main causes of it. The first one is through the fault of the parents, and the other is through the fault of the siblings. As for the discord produced by the fault of the parents, we have already talked enough about it. For the other, it happens when the brothers are more concerned with the parts than with the whole body. What I mean by the body, is all the brothers together, and by the parts, each one of them. The brothers are on par with our eyes, hands, and feet. If we examine the matter thoroughly, we shall find that the brothers are more capable of helping each other than the parts of our body. One hand can only help the other hand when it is present, and one foot the other foot that is next to it. The mutual aid of brothers goes much further. Even when they are separated from one another, they do not cease to assist and help each other. Therefore, if the brothers, according to their nature, devoted themselves primarily to the conversation of this body, without devoting their sole care to their particular part, there would be no doubt about their sibling love and good agreement together.

William. Indeed, the bad passion of bearing great affection for ourselves does not allow us to love others as we should, even if they are never that close to us.

Anniball. This is true and why there are very few brothers who put honor and the common good before their interest. Every day we see common things neglected. While a brother devotes to the care of himself, their strength is weakened. If each one withdraws his part, confines it in his heart, in such a way that he no longer has any thought of the other, he tends to be selfish in everything, which ordinarily follows the ruin and the shame of the family. This was clearly shown by that wise father who, with a bundle of rods, helped his children understand how invincible their strength was, as long as they stood together. For this reason, it is necessary that the brothers, above all else, should place honor and the common good above all things. All of them, both in deeds and in conversation, must take care to preserve the honor of their family. None of them should be persuaded by their virtue alone that they can make up for the lack of the others and still bring back honor to the family.

William. Please, as long as I live virtuously and well, do you think my honor is compromised, even if some of my brothers live badly?

Anniball. Your particular honor will not be diminished, but the common honor of your family, which you are a part of, will be.

William. Why would my commendable behavior not counteract their lewd demeanor?

Anniball. However much you may counteract

it, you cannot erase the dishonor your family suffers, which receives as much shame from the bad deeds as it does honor from the good ones. For this reason, they are mostly to blame when they do not care for their siblings as much as themselves. For the families' well-being, as we have said members of one body, one of them cannot be stained alone without the whole body being spotted. This is the reason why it is said, *"You cannot cut off the nose without bloodying the mouth."* This closeness that must exist between brothers is also implied in the name of brother, which in Latin signifies as if he were another, to help us understand that a brother to a brother is like another of himself. Therefore, I cannot give a clearer example than of a work or book, of which various volumes are printed in a press, which perhaps differs in cover and outer covering, and yet are one thing, having one beginning and one end. Any defects that are in one of these volumes are common to all of them; hence I deduce that the fault which is in one brother is common to all the others. Therefore, for the honor of their family, brothers should support one another. When one falls, the other must help him up or else confess that he has fallen to the ground. Besides, it is improper for a man to see himself raised to a high degree, and to look down upon his brother in an inferior state. One may dare to say that if someone does not care for the honor of their sibling, does not care for their own honor.

Scipio Africanus[53] was very mindful of this common honor. After having subdued Spain, defeated Hannibal,[54] and conquered Africa, he thought that he had done nothing if he did not see the honor and fame of his brother rise as well. Being so jealous of this he not only saw to it that his brother was chosen by the people of Rome for the enterprise in Asia, but he ended up depriving himself of his authority because he was content in following him as a man-at-arms and as a private soldier, honoring him openly like a general and secretly advising him like a brother. He worked so well with him that the honor he bestowed on his brother, encouraged by the advice he gave and the example he set, earned his brother the name of Asiaticus,[55] to his immortal glory and the singular benefit of the people of Rome.

William. Asiaticus might well have said about Africanus.

> *He was my father in honor, my son in love,*
> *and my brother in years.*

Truly it was a notable love, and worthy of eternal remembrance, to the shame of those who are so far from procuring the honor and advancement of their brothers, that they rejoice in their misery and misfortune.

Anniball. I could cite many examples of such

Brothers

brothers who, because of malice and discord, were led so awry continually seeking to dishonor one another, and were both shamed, causing some to mock and others to pity them. It is a thing worthy of praise and admiration to see the agreement and friendship established among brothers so that none of them does anything for their convenience but with the consent of the others for the common honor and advancement of their family. As long as the bond of brotherhood is tied in this way, it may well be said that the sword that untied Gordian's knot[56] will not be able to undo it.

In short, there is nothing that maintains the honor of a family so much as the agreement between brothers. I must say that these families are much happier and more fortunate where several brothers get along well together, than where there is only one. No one has the strength of Atlas to carry the sky with his shoulders, so there is no burden so heavy that is supported by several does not become light. Since the nature, degrees, and professions of the brothers are diverse, and each one of them puts all his care into the advancement of his family, they will apply themselves diligently, like the workmen of a building, some by instruction, others by arms, some by temporal or spiritual promotions, others by some profitable business of life, or by some other means; all things that cannot be in one person.

Civil Conversation III

William. Now that you have shown how necessary agreement is among brothers, I would like you to establish some rules for conversation that will allow them to maintain it.

Anniball. The form of their conversation depends, first of all, on the prudence and authority of the father, who must endeavor to keep them united together in love and encourage them to honor and help one another. After they have reached the age of understanding, it is their duty, living in common, to beware of ascribing anything particular to themselves nor be suspicious of each other. Besides the offense to God and fame, nothing would cause disdain or ill will with each other than this. Furthermore, it behooves them to observe the order of nature so that the younger, if there is no inequality of degree, shall do honor to his elder brother. A custom introduced by the Romans among friends should always take place among siblings that the elder brother is not entirely free because it behooves him to reward the humility of his younger brother with so much goodwill and liberality that he has more desire to render honor to him. The elder brother must have more discretion and bear with the younger brother when he fails in the duties of his older brother. He should help him understand his fault with gentleness and in due time so that his advice is not taken wrong and may be regarded as proceeding from goodwill so that his brother may bear greater affection toward him. Above all, I think it is necessary to maintain concord among brothers living together. They should not be too bold with each other, through words or deeds, which often starts arguments between them. They should show such modest respect in their actions so dislike does not have to grow.

William. On the one hand, I like this recollection because the excessive liberty of words and customs without restraints sometimes causes such a deep wound that the pain is intolerable. One will resent it with the tongue and sometimes with their hands. On the other hand, by using this respect you have spoken about, the brothers will not dare to use the corrections and warnings for fear of offending one another. Hence, it follows what the poet said,

Woe to him who contrasts, woe to him who hides.[57]

Anniball. I disagree, and in my opinion, it is quite the opposite. The rebuke from a foul-mouthed person lacks any great force and is rather imputed to their horrible nature than any desire they may have to make amends with their brother. The advice from a discreet man is well accepted, and the party who receives it is convinced that it is for a great cause and goodwill that the other, being so wise and so honest, uses it. You must not think that mentioning modest respect means a distrustful fear that prevents us from speaking the truth freely, such as the fashion towards princes, magistrates, and superiors. This fear would altogether quench the fire of love that is necessary between good brothers. I meant that the grave and discreet manner by which we honor others causes others to do honor to us. This enables us not to reprehend our friend, much less our brother.

William. However, I think some brothers refrain from doing so for fear of offending one another, just as servants are afraid to speak to their masters.

Anniball. Instead, let's say that the lack of goodwill keeps them from doing so. Hence, one brother does not seek to amend the other, but delights in slandering him.

William. Our reverend brother Bernardin Maccia, a reader of the Institutes, mentioned this, recounting that he had known two brothers. One was a student and the other a courtier. Although they were considered honest men, it was hard to spend time with them because they were so talkative. One day he had the opportunity to go and visit the student who was not feeling well. As he entered the house, he met the other brother who was coming out and asked how his sick brother was doing. The latter answered, *"Reasonably well, but please go and see him. I guarantee he will tire you out with his babbling."* After entering the room and expressing many words of comfort to the sick man, he said, *"I shall not ask you how your brother is since I just saw him very merry as I was coming in."* The sick man replied, *"Men who have the world at will, like him, are never sad and if you had been with him long, he would have made you deaf with his prattling."*

Anniball. To tell the truth, if brothers agreed to tell each other their faults in private, they would avoid the mockery and ridicule of others openly. It seems to me that we have spoken enough of this matter. We can conclude that as one hand washes another and both face each other, each brother should support the other, so they all can procure honor for their family. To maintain this, there must be concord composed of love, discretion, honorable respect, and friendly reproach is required among them.

Masters and servants

William. As far as I can see, we are on the verge of concluding our discourse since we have nothing else to discuss, but the conversation between the master and the servant. I fear it may be burdensome for you to spend time here, to your detriment, when you could employ that time to your advantage elsewhere.

Anniball. I frequent other places to please others, and I do indeed pass my time there. I am with you for my pleasure. Therefore, I have found the time to be here. Let's go forward cheerfully. If my servant is not visibly distressed when assisting me while I am here, it is not possible to find a master and servant more contented than we are.

William. I will answer for your man who is content with where he is now. He is with our servants who spend time together in three things in which they take a singular pleasure.

Anniball. What are they?

William. Drinking, gambling, and bad language.

Anniball. These things can only be done to the detriment and disgrace of the masters.

William. Even if they would have these three things, I guarantee your man is content since he is out of your sight.

Anniball. I believe this even without an oath. Where do you think this content from the servants comes from?

William. From lack of love. If they loved their master, they would love his presence and stand with him.

Anniball. Where do you think this lack of love comes from?

William. Perhaps from the difference in life, mind, and manner between them. What do you think?

Anniball. I also have this opinion, but servitude may be a source of this lack of love (not to say hatred) from servants toward their masters. Men commonly serve more out of necessity than out of free will. If a man knows he is born free when he puts himself into service, he constrains his nature. Even though he voluntarily makes himself a prisoner, it cannot be said that he is pleased or does not hate the one who keeps him in subjection. No doubt about it, but even though he has promised and sworn fidelity to his master, in his heart, he rebels against his service. Therefore, it is no wonder that he flees from his presence and prefers to be his servant from a distance than serve him nearby. As long as he is out of his master's sight, he somewhat forgets that he is a servant and thinks he has recovered his freedom. On the contrary, when he stands before his master, he lowers his head and persuades himself that he has returned to his collar like a dog that has been let loose for a time.

William. It is good that we come to the distinction of servants here. What you say about servants who flee from the presence of their master is not the norm and should be understood for the nature of vile and lowly servants. The better sort, the ones who are gentlemen, for the most part, are never pleased except when they are in the presence of the master and serve him lovingly and willingly. It is said, *"The gentleman loves, and the slave fears."*

Anniball. The distinction that can be made between courtier gentlemen who serve princes, and people of low status, who serve gentlemen, is that the chains or fetters of people of low status are made of iron, and those of gentlemen are made of gold.

William. I agree with this difference and acknowledge that chains of gold bind more strongly than ones made of iron. I do not think you can say that gentlemen and common servants serve with one mind or propose to themselves the end of their service.

Anniball. I will tell you, common servants hate both their master and the chain, while the others love their masters, but cannot do without the chain.

William. I do not see how it can be said that gentlemen cannot do without the chain. They do not seek amusements out of compulsion or necessity as baser sorts do. They are naturally inclined to do so for honor and renown and do not seek to impose themselves for vile gain like others do. I will not speak of others, but only myself. I assure you that the Duke, my master, seeing that I am unfit to serve him because of my illness, gave me a better pension to live on, from now on within my house, than I had when I was in his court. Yet, to confess my ambition to you, when I live in my father's house, I shall be no more than my other neighbors and consider myself no use to the world. Whereas being near the prince, I can please several people every hour, make friends every day, and be honored by the most honorable of the court. I curse my infirmity, which will not allow me to be bound to this golden chain I love above all things in this world.

Anniball. All men endowed with a noble soul love that chain, not for itself, but for the honor attached to it. I remember hearing your brother say he loved my lady, his mistress, but could not wallow away in service. I can tell you that he would have taken his head out of the collar of these unbearable pains long before the death of this princess had not her extreme kindness and extraordinary favors towards him prevented him. In truth, this constraint to eat, speak, and go by the mouth, tongue, and feet of others; this property of having never rest either in body or spirit, to slacken in the service of his master. To be brief, these inconveniences, vexations, troubles, and annoyances described in one of your letters, which you have endured firsthand for some time, fill the cup with a potion so bitter that its odor, indeed, the mere recollection of it, offends nature.

William. You know well that a man does not win the bet without running.

Anniball. Yet you know that many run, but there is only one winner. The one rewarded for his services will hear many complain that they have consumed their goods and risked their

Masters and servants

lives in the service of princes without gaining anything more than a miserable old age. With their repentance too late, few will feel the suffering from harsh labor or grief. This golden chain has never appealed to me, and I have always considered all service unsatisfactory and miserable. The one exception is the service of a Spanish gentleman who, once serving his king for a long time, became a monk. He immediately wrote to the king that he preferred the service of a superior prince whom he expected better wages than he received from the hands of his master. These servants, who enter into the ministry and service of God, no doubt love the master and the chain well and are the only ones who devote themselves to service. Since our purpose is to discuss this earthly and uncertain service by returning to the gentlemen who serve men, I grant, for the most part, they love their masters to whom they are similar in life, mind, and manners. Therefore, they think they are happy in their presence and when they are offered the opportunity of some adequate service. Some servants withdraw themselves as much as possible from the sight of their masters, so they can avoid doing anything. On the contrary, the better ones consider themselves in better favor when employed more than their fellows are.

William. Princes are better served for no other

reason than we are, but only because their servants are gentlemen and ours are not. Now seems like a good time to discuss the conversation between master and servant.

Anniball. Let's always follow the rule we have observed in our discussion and first show the origin of the discords and inconveniences that arise among them daily. Then we can seek the means to make everything right and get them to agree.

William. I believe this has already been stated on one occasion when we mentioned the difference between their lives and their ways.

Anniball. What you say is true, but this occasion is common to the master and the servant. There are two others; one depends on the master, the other on the servant. It is incumbent for one to command and the other to serve. Therefore, if one of them fails in his duty, trouble and disorder develop between them. The master commits a fault when he does not know how to command, and that is why the philosopher said, *"The master must first know how to command the things that the servant must do; but it is not as easy to know how to command, as is it is to be a master."*

William. Therefore, you must prescribe to the master the way to command.

Anniball. The way is established if he serves before he commands, that is, if he learns to serve before he begins to command.

William. I have this opinion as well. I consider it impossible that if you have never had a master, you can not know how to do it well. For this reason, I would not exchange the Duke, my master, for the Emperor because he was accustomed from childhood to rendering continuous service, first to King Henry, then King Francis, King Charles, his children, and successors in the kingdom. He knows how important it is to possess the hearts and minds of his servants using a wise and gentle command over his gentlemen. I have noticed two successful effects from the service he renders himself. First, enduring a lot of labor both in mind and body, he knows firsthand the pain of his servants. So moved by pity, he looks upon them with a more accommodating eye and commands them more gently. The other is because, although he is a great prince and can live at ease, his servants, seeing him serve continually, are driven by his example to render obedience to him regardless of the pain they endure while in his service.

Anniball. Truthfully, he shows himself to be such a worthy and courteous prince that he has more servants throughout Europe than in his court. These times are so unfortunate because there is no one like Homer[58] to describe the exploits of such an Achilles[59]. Returning now to the fault of the masters, we will say once more that only those who can obey well can command well. Since few masters can do so, in almost every house, one finds indiscreet, proud, fanciful, and insolent masters who ask nothing of their servants, but to be slaves. They speak to them arrogantly, never content, unless they see them trembling in their presence, using speech full of terrifying threats and insults.

William. In this way, servants, though well-founded and sufficient, begin to become useless, grow cold in their goodwill, and remiss in their duties. These masters are more indiscreet and fight and quarrel with their servants in front of strangers. From my perspective, they make strangers believe they are unwelcome in their house and maliciously spite their servants. As proof of this, when a servant seeks a master, he never inquires whether he is covetous or of bad character but whether he is cruel and difficult to please.

Anniball. Even worse are those who turn on their servants with their hands, who probably have been beaten by their masters if they have served, and thus take revenge on their servants. Perhaps, they convince themselves that their servants cannot help themselves with their daggers, which I have seen an example of in Padua. In truth, there is nothing that makes me angrier than this. I can only think ill thoughts of those who tyrannically triumph over their poor servants. They should refrain from injuring them just as they would their equals. It is an act of great kindness to guard against oppressing those who can be easily victimized. Therefore, it is in the best interest of a wise master to refrain from beating their servants. They should remember that the supreme master will not be pleased with him taking revenge from his hands. The punishment of his servants should not be left to him and his divine pleasure unless it is for crimes punished by human laws. Other masters of this disposition will have their servants understand their minds by only making a sign as if they were dumb and their servant's soothsayers. Some make their servants do three or four things at once without having the judgment to consider, as one sexton[60] said, "*A man cannot carry the cross and ring the bells at the same time.*" Some are so curious that if they had a thousand servants, they would trouble them all and never be satisfied. None of the servants would be able to please them because their fashion is to change servants every month.

William. About six months ago, we had a gentleman at court who gave one of his servants a livery coat which he later gave to four others and then took back from them. Shortly before we departed from France, he sent his servant to me in the evening to ask me for a favor to write a letter in the name of the Duke concerning some of his affairs. The following morning a different man came to retrieve the letter, and I told him that he was not the same as yesterday. He answered, *"Even though I am not him, I am wearing his clothes, which my master had taken off his back this morning for me to wear."*

Anniball. In my opinion, this is a disgraceful thing to do. Although it is not dishonorable for the master to undress Peter to clothe Paul, it is at least a disgrace for him to change his servants so often. This shows him to be an impatient and challenging man to please while he spreads his secrets and business far and wide. When a servant leaves his master for whatever reason, whether he is pleased or displeased, he cannot refrain from reporting wherever he goes the life and behavior of his former master. Even if he mixes the truth with a hundred lies, some will believe him. Besides this, the master will have a tough time getting his new servants to adjust to his way of doing business.

Among the other horrible masters, some are so impatient and unreasonable that they impose impossible tasks on their servants, demanding things at their hands before they have even been commanded. The worst of all are those who wrongfully burden their servants with some bad business and then let them go, keeping their sweets and the ones that are due them for it.

William. It's easy to find a stick to beat a dog

with.

Anniball. It would be too long to list all the imperfections of those masters who never served.

William. Yes, but those same ones who have served and do serve daily are servants to their own vices.

Anniball. I agree with your statement. Let's turn to disagreements between the master and servant that occurs when servants are incapable of serving and obeying. Being incapable of service, I not only mean the fools and ignorant asses; but the dishonest and cunning companions. Even though they are sufficient to perform everything entrusted to them, they have some notable defects for which their masters are justified in dismissing them. It is as hard to find servants without faults as a patient sick from dropsy suffering from thirst. Though their mistakes are innumerable, their main qualities are the three properties of a dog, starting with the throat because they are gluttonous. Next comes barking, even when the master does nothing because they immediately report it to everyone. Like the servant showed in a comedy by saying that he was full of holes because of everything that came into his ears. Last but not least, biting, which is so natural to them that their masters never do any good to them. They will not refrain from calling them ungrateful and saying the worst words from their bellies, per the poet's saying,

Of the sorry servants, the worst part is the tongue.

They are worse than dogs, including the properties just mentioned. They are proud and arrogant, making one say,

Of surly servants, every court is full.

This vice is accompanied by lying (being the most abject thing of all), and they frame themselves never to tell the truth to their masters, nor even to their ghostly fathers. This would be a small matter if their unfaithfulness were not so great that they are not only content to take money to be disbursed from their masters and appropriate it for themselves but are not faithful in matters that touch their honor and credit. I conclude that their slightest fault deserves the galley[61] according to the saying, *"We have as many enemies as we have servants."* By this, we must understand the lowest and most rascally types, for it can not be said, *"There are good masters, so there are also good servants."*

William. I believe it is good, but to eliminate all disorder, the good master and good servant must get along. If they are both not good, it is difficult for the wisdom of one to make up for the lack of discretion in the other.

Anniball. I think so, but we must remember what we have previously said since the golden world has disappeared. Master and servant must understand there is no absolute perfection in any person. Some imperfections must be endured so the best and most necessary parts are not lacking. This consideration must be made not only by the servant by remembering he must submit to the master's will and pleasure. The master must also do it more knowingly than the servants having nasty conditions that are naturally inclined to do bad things and will not have that fidelity, diligence, and affection they would have towards a prince. It would be in his best interest to close his eyes to some faults of the servants rather than go through the trouble of reforming them.

William. So please tell me what imperfections should be tolerated in servants.

Anniball. Your demand reminds me of a mistake I committed the other day in repeating the imperfections of others. What I said of tolerable men is that they generally suffer from this exception. This does not extend to the people of the household, who are under the jurisdiction of the master of the house. He should not open the way of vices to those who he can stop, but be more severe towards himself than toward others, like the example of Cato, who said, "*He forgave all but himself.*" It may be stated that their faults belong to the master. If the proverbs are true, "*Like master, like man*" and

Civil Conversation III

"The fish rots from the head," there is no doubt that the faults of our servants will fall on us. Either because we have instructed them or we take pleasure in their misbehavior. The servant will be intolerable to his master because of those imperfections. On the other hand, these faults are tolerated by others, so much so that the master should not put up with him, but let him go or make him correct his faults.

William. I doubt if you want to restrict the rules of servants and the obligations of masters too much. When the father, who is occupied in other matters, has his children instructed by masters and governors, there is no reason why he should become the teacher of his servants who are naturally inclined to do bad things that he would have much to do in redressing them. If he does this, he becomes the servant and not them. As for me, I have other things to do than watch my servants, so I am assured that they are not up to no good.

Anniball. I know for a fact that some servants, in the presence of their masters, look as if butter would not melt in their mouths. When out of their sight will kindly play their parts and will not make fun of their master behind his back. The master must in no way allow his servants to commit, either by word or deed, any fault that may dishonor God himself or his neighbor, making it clear to them that he does not tolerate any wickedness in his house and that he detests this behavior. This way, even if he cannot eradicate their wicked behavior, he will at least make them pretend to be honest for fear of displeasing him.

Touching on other minor natural imperfections, such as rudeness, indiscretion, foolishness, carelessness, forgetfulness, cunning, querulousness, spitefulness, gluttony, importunity, laziness, boastfulness, and the like, should be endured if they cannot be eliminated. In my view, I think such servants are better lost than found, and the house is the worse for it the more they are in it. Yet I know some honest gentlemen who, as long as their servants are faithful and trustworthy, do not care that they are fools, boasters, or jesters, to entertain themselves.

William. In Paris, there was a gentleman who, while leaving his house, asked his servant to go to a butcher named David to buy him some tripe. The servant returned after discovering that the butcher had sold all the tripe. The master was in the church at the time listening to a sermon, and by chance, as the servant entered the church, the preacher (who intended to quote some scripture text from the Psalms of David) said, *"What does David say?"* *"Mary,"* said the servant, *"he has sold all the tripe."* I am not sure whether that should be called foolishness or pleasantness.

Anniball. There are also some masters who, when their servants mock and ridicule them, take pleasure in it, then seem angry with them. Like the one who called his servant the King of Fools, the servant answered, "*I would like to be the King of Fools. I would no doubt rule over them better than myself.*"

William. I could not play the philosopher like that with my servants.

Anniball. Nor could I. Perhaps that servant was productive for him, and he was content to bear this mockery. All masters are not so meek-minded to be served by such men or servants so happy to meet masters who may like them. Let's establish an order so that the master and servant may live and get along quietly together.

William. That's what I want to hear.

Anniball. First, I consider it necessary that someone who desires to be well served should require three particular things from their servant; namely, love, faithfulness, and sufficiency. This master will easily find if he disposes himself to be a good and loving master, following the commandment of the wise man, "*Love him whom thou nourishes,*" which he will be compelled to do only if he thinks that the servants, even if they serve, are men, dwell with us, are our humble friends, and our fellow servants. Therefore, he will know he must live with them with kindness and familiarity. This will earn him the goodwill of his servants, and he will know that the author of this saying, "*As many servants so many enemies,*"[62] meant perhaps to accuse the master and not the servants. We do not receive them as enemies, but make them so by our misuse.

William. Yes, but consider how those who put this precept into practice find the opposite of what you say and find out too late that nothing makes the servant more insolent and glorious than the excessive kindness of the master. You know the proverb well,

> *Claw a clown, and he will scratch you.*
> *Scratch a clown, and he will claw you.*

For my part, I cannot make my servants my companions to be too familiar with them. I like to love them but not embrace them.

Anniball. We must set limits and boundaries for all our actions, which we must not exceed. I agree with you that the master should keep his state and degree. If, as you say, he is well-known to his servant, he would show himself low-minded, unfit for fellowship, and be like a servant with servants, which would be to his discredit. Moreover, he would soon find that too much familiarity breeds contempt. That is why men of better judgment conduct themselves with their servants in some way so that they are not so saucy by too much familiarity nor too fearful by too much severity.

Under no circumstances should a master be terrible to his servant by disapproving of him, making him think that he does not love him and does not like his service, which is the best way to discourage him. Yet, in giving his servant a just countenance, he must take care to observe the proper time and place. If I may say so, he must have two faces imitating the sun, which in the course of its journey through the sky for a moment shows a face covered with clouds, the other when these misty vapors are driven away, and it shows itself clear and bright. Just as it seems when the master is abroad and is in the presence of strangers casts a grave and sad look upon his servants. It is his duty when he retires to his own house to look upon them more pleasantly and speak to them more familiarly. Servants love this best and are encouraged to render good service.

If the master is a gentleman and remembers his time while serving some prince, he should recollect how happy the courtiers were when a good word or some small favor came from their prince. You can now see how a master with his honor shows courtesy to his servants and thus obtains their goodwill and love. This will enable him to purchase their loyalty and fidelity, a necessary thing for his honor and profit. For so much as sufficiency, as we have said, must be united with love and devotion, the master must be entrusted, in this regard, with instructing his servant.

William. Then you will make the master a schoolmaster for his servant.

Anniball. No, but for himself because he should learn to command. If he can command well, he will be well served. He should also not persuade himself that his servants should discharge him of all his affairs. He should participate with them and consider that it is not easy to govern servants. The more servants he has, the more difficulty he has guiding them. When there are many servants, there is a lot of quarreling and contention in the house.

William. What is the best way to command

well?

Anniball. There are two things, one lies in words, the other in deeds. Touching on the first, he must think that there is no servant so well-prepared from the service of another master(s) that he would be unwilling to receive new instructions. The servant needs to know how he will proceed in his actions so that he will do nothing contrary to the master's will and pleasure. Therefore, he must not think at the first sight of trouble his servant is made to bow to his way. He must calmly and patiently make him understand his thoughts and speak freely to help him abandon his old ways, which he may not like, and to frame him to his manner in doing things. If I were to take a servant, I would choose a freshwater soldier, who has never served, than one who has served for a long time. Those who have served in many houses have mostly picked up some bad habits and can rarely give them up. One who has never been a servant is more easily led, gentle, and fit for every type of service. Generally, the master will be more pleased with his goodwill than with the skill of the others.

William. I agree with you because it is too difficult to change the manners of an old servant, who would sooner change his hairstyle than his habits. Yet, for a time, one must be willing to use a lot of patience and take great pains with a young servant.

Anniball. This is true, but to have less trouble, choose one of good capacity and suitable for service.

William. Count Hector Miroglio, our friend, once had the opportunity to test the sensible wit of a new servant. Having sent his other servants on other business and after having him prepare the house, he asked him to cover the table, which he did. Although on that particular day, he was dining alone in his room, his servant put two plates on the table and two stools across from each other. The Count said nothing, suspecting his intentions, and waited to see what he would do. After the meat was brought in, as soon as his man had given him water, he sat down, which he had not yet done. His man, having already washed up, sat down opposite of him. The Count, as you know, naturally inclined to cheerfulness, kept his composure and left his man alone. After eating together for a while, the man wondered if his master might be thirsty and said, "*Master, when you want to drink, please do me the courtesy of not ordering me to do so.*" The Count laughed so heartily that the poor fool, knowing his mistake, got up to fetch him a drink but did not sit down anymore.

Anniball. In my opinion, this country does not produce good servants.

William. I think the cause is that in this place, the princes seldom hold their courts where the servants mainly learn good behavior. Besides, our nature is such that we make ourselves more familiar with our servants than they do in other places and we do not care to be served honorably, orderly, and respectfully. Hence, the servants are unskillful and rude in their behavior.

Anniball. However, I must say that not all of our servants are very civilized, faithful, and trustworthy, which is more important than civility, finesse, or bravery. Therefore, to return to our purpose, we see that the master who wants to be well served should not spare his words, either to command what he wants to be done or to gently instruct his servant in what he is ignorant of, pointing out his faults.

Having spoken of the master's commands in words, we must discuss their commands in deeds. The master commands his servant in things, often by his example and actions he wants him to imitate. Therefore, if he wants his servant to be careful and diligent in his service, he must be equally cautious in his affairs. There is nothing more than the diligence of the master that awakens servants. On the other hand, servants can not be diligent if the master is negligent. In this regard, it is said, "*The eye of the master fattens the horse.*" [63] In this regard, a philosopher was asked, "*Which manure was more useful for the fields?*" He replied, "*Let the master walk around the fields often so the servants can have hope that it seems to be a small effort while they see him occupied in similar or other exercises."*

Moreover, he can expect they will follow him in shameful and praiseworthy things. He must be as fearful of giving them a bad example as he is careful to give them a good one.

The master also commands well when he knows how to use his authority in such a way that he is better served by averting his gaze than others who, by insulting and threatening words, make the whole house tremble, not knowing as the poet says,

Great strength is hidden in gentle sovereignty.

Therefore, masters must be careful not to contradict the saying, "*I do not want to trouble my servants like a lion, nor oppress them.*"

Now, when the Master knows that he has obtained the love, fidelity, and sufficiency of his servant; he must take care in every way to preserve what he has acquired because there is nothing more effective than to use him courteously. Helping him in his troubles, visiting him in his sicknesses, and granting him, when the occasion calls for it, what will cost the master little and please the servant much. This way, the servant does not think he is indebted to his Master for the wages of his labor but only for what he will generously grant him out of courtesy. That Master, whether a gentleman or not, is greatly deceived when he thinks his servant serves him only for wages without hope of any other reward. Therefore, do not forget to reward the good servant and keep him always with you as a precious thing; remembering that the servant is, in a sense, a part of the master and that there is nothing more necessary in this life than a good servant. Wherefore it is written, "*If you have a trustworthy servant, let him be to you as your own soul.*" The master should not think it is beneath him to listen to his reasons, consult with him, and govern himself according to his faithful counsel. There have been servants found that advance and make the master's house more profitable than his brothers or sons.

In conclusion, the master should use his servant with familiarity, remembering to treat his inferiors as he would like to be treated by his superiors. In this way, bearing this in mind, he will always avoid the detestable vice of ingratitude. As he increases his capacity, he will improve the condition of his servant. In addition to the promised salary, he will not fail to reward generously, according to his power, the long and loyal services he has rendered him.

William. As far as I can see, you have instructed both the master and servant that it would not seem wrong that the servant should be given some special charge.

Anniball. I charge the servant to learn the meaning of this old proverb,

Making the dog's bed is difficult.

Just as one cannot tell on which side the dog will lay when they turn around to get ready to lie down, a servant cannot determine what service may be acceptable and agreeable to his master when, for the most part, it is variable and diverse. Therefore, the master being of such a delicate nature, he must determine to endure endless labor in serving him, which he will hardly be able to satisfy himself. He must be cautious not to incur the common error of servants, who like new brooms which clean the house well, serve diligently at first, then slacken. This is not the way to gain favor. The reward does not belong to the one who begins but to the one who perseveres.

The servant must assume that his master is waiting for him to turn up sooner than to become intemperate in serving. A servant must also conform all of his thoughts and actions to the will and pleasure of his master and tie the ass, as they say, where the master wants him to be bound without any contradiction. Nothing displeases a man more than seeing those who should obey him resist him. He should not seek to gain credit with his master by flattery or hypocrisy but let him serve and obey him with a sincere heart. Through feigned words, he will build an argument for unfaithful deeds, whereby his master is continually suspicious. He must remember that the servant needs knowledge more than speech. At any rate, he should not forget anything other than this, that is, to serve faithfully not out of fear of his master's power but out of his own debt. A fellow wisely answered someone who said, "*If I take you into my service will you be an honest man?*" "*Yes,*" he answered, "*even if you do not take me.*"

All service is poorly applied, which is not well accepted, and there is no greater sorrow than to serve and not be able to please. When he sees that he cannot conform to his master's wishes he should seek to leave his house with good graces, then remain with poor satisfaction. When he sees that he is in his master's favor let him stay saying in his heart, "*Happy is he who serves the happy.*" He does not seek to change, remembering, "*A rolling stone gathers no moss.*" To make it short, let him not lack love, reverence, faithfulness, diligence, wariness, readiness, or secrecy. Let him disregard his own life in the service of his master, following the common saying, "*To serve like a doe, or flee like a stag.*"

William. It occurs to me that we did not order our things as we should have because we talked about the conversation of private masters with the lowest kind of servants. In contrast, we should have spoken about the conversation between a prince and the courtier first.

Anniball. We said yesterday that princes do not need our instructions therefore, it is not necessary to prescribe to them any orders as to how to entertain their entourage. They conduct themselves in their courts honorably, peaceably, and quietly. They do not injure their servants either by words or deeds. Those disturbances commonly seen in private homes are not seen in the courts of princes. In short, they are in all respects impeccable.

William. Since you are so reluctant, whatever the matter, to establish any form of conversation with the princes, please prescribe some orders, at least to their servants, so that our discourse will in any way not be imperfect.

Anniball. Since it's getting late, and I have just been called away to other business, you know we are eased off this discussion by the one whose learned pen formed *The Book of the Courtier* most perfectly.[64]

William. That gentleman, by the excellence of that work, has no doubt earned immortal fame, nor has he omitted anything that belongs to the duties of a proper courtier.

A prescription for health

William. Before your departure, I would like you to observe the order of a diligent physician who notwithstanding the prescriptions of other physicians, does not fail to give one of his own to the patient.

Anniball. I will give you two prescriptions if one is insufficient because it would be wrong to propose simple and ordinary things to gentlemen, namely, love, faith, diligence, and reverence, which are due to princes. I give this remedy to a courtier since the prince, as we said yesterday, is an earthly God. It is fitting to honor him always as a sacred thing. Remember when the Athenians denied Alexander divine honors, this voice was heard, though hardly Christian, *"Take heed while you behold heaven, you do not lose the earth."* This is the first remedy. The second is

A prescription for health

composed of two medicines that I have taken from the recipe book of an excellent philosopher. Either one or both, if the courtier uses them, may keep himself long in favor of his prince; they are abstinence or food seasoned with sugar.

William. Could you please explain your remedy more clearly?

Annibal. I will do it in these two verses.

Before their Prince the courtier is silent,
or their words are sauced with pleasant glee.

William. Oh, how short pleasures are. I did not know it was so late. Now, after the delicate meats that you have made me taste these three days, I hope that tomorrow you will be pleased to close my stomach with that snack or banquet that you have already promised me. Therefore, with this sugar in my mouth, I can leave the day after tomorrow for the Duke, my master, who by his letters, has sent for me on some important business.

Annibal. I shall be with you tomorrow. Not as you say to sweeten your mouth, but to take leave of you. This will be very sorrowful to me were it not that you have given me hope of your speedy return.

William. I do not doubt that you are pleased with my presence because you know that I honor your singular virtues. You may also think that the pleasure I receive from your presence is much better because the patient needs the physician more than the physician needs the patient. I will not say that I need you more to be healed, but to preserve the health I have recovered by your means.

Anniball. I sense from our conversations that you are more of a physician than a patient.

William. You are not ignorant of how, in this illness, I used solitude instead of a remedy so that I could only choose to shorten my days. Then showed me my error by which I wished to make myself a grave and taught me to discern good company from bad. You reminded me of the general points that all men should observe in their conduct. Then the particular points that are appropriate to each one in conversation and company, as well as abroad, and at home. I feel my heart and soul healed. I dare say that I have recovered my health.

Anniball. I know that I have not entirely satisfied you or myself in these discourses, but I am sure you are not mistaken in saying that civil conversation greatly helps the infirmity of the mind. Nothing in the world teaches us more wit or manners, stimulates us more to do well, or restrains us from doing horrible things than companionship and conversation with good and virtuous people. Do not be deceived by saying that the health of the body often comes from the health of the mind. Galen says that restlessness

A prescription for health

of the mind begets sickness of the body and that he has cured many illnesses by restoring the pulse to good health and soothing the mind. I am not as skilled as I ought to be in curing diseased minds, knowing that I need medicine. I will be here tomorrow to delight you, though I cannot do you any good.

William. I will wait for you with great anticipation. I beg you to please come sooner than you did today.

The end of the third book.

Bibliography

Guazzo, Stefano. The Civile Conversation. Translated by Pettie, George. First Volume. New York, New York: AMS Press, Inc., 1925.

Guazzo, Stefano. La Civil Conversatione. First Volume. Brescia, Italy: Appresso Tomaso Bozzola, 1574.

Florio, John. Queen Anna's New World of Words, or Dictionare of the Italian and English Tongues. London, 1611.

"Dante Lab at Dartmouth College: Reader". Dante Lab at Dartmouth College. http://dantelab.dartmouth.edu/reader

"Wikipedia." Wikipedia. www.wikipedia.org. https://www.wikipedia.org/.

"Dictionary by Merriam-Webster: America's Most-trusted Online Dictionary." Dictionary by Merriam-Webster: America's most-trusted

Notes

online dictionary. www.merriam-webster.com. https://www.merriam-webster.com/.

"Thesaurus by Merriam-Webster." Thesaurus by Merriam-Webster: More than Synonyms and Antonyms. www.merriam-webster.com. https://www.merriam-webster.com/thesaurus.

"Quotes of famous people" by Quotepark s.r.o. www.quotepark.com. https://quotepark.com/quotes/902210-homer-few-sons-indeed-are-like-their-fathers-general/.

Index

Absalom, 108
Aeneas, 107
Africa, 136
Africanus, 136
Agnolo (Angelo)
　Ambrogini, 125
Alessio (Alexis)
　Piemontese, 19
Alexander, 23, 78
Amazons, 126
Amnon, 109
Aristippus, 92
Aristotle, 78, 125
Ascanius, 107
Asia, 136
Asiaticus, 136
Atlas, 137
Baldassare Castiglione, 169
Baptista Spagnuoli
　Mantuanus, 13
Battle of Saint-
　Quinten, 131
Boccaccio, 119
Caesar Augustus, 76
Caspians, 98
Cato, 43, 76, 82, 125
Charles V, 102
Christ, 38, 67, 81
Christian, 38, 45, 80, 107
Crates, 22
Cremona, 77
cuckoos, 74
Dante, 69, 174
Demetrius, 50

Index

devil, 6, 21, 34, 127
Devil, 48
Diogenes, 77
distaff, 113
Ecclesiasticus 33:19, 102
Egypt, 102
Eteocles, 129
France, 8, 23, 71, 118, 119
Galen, 72
Genoa, 1, 2
God, 9, 18, 21, 22, 23, 32, 45, 47, 49, 51, 59, 62, 67, 70, 80, 81, 86, 104, 109, 124
Gordian knot, 137
Gracchi, 72
Hannibal, 136
harlot, 21, 54
Hecuba, 18
Helen, 38, 113
Helena, 18
Hercole Strozzi, 130
Herod, 16
Holofernes, 127
Hypsicratea, 62
Italian, 130, 174, 179
Italians, 124
James 1:6, 38

Judith, 127
Juno, 13
King David, 108
King of the Winds, 13
Lady Cornelia, 101
Laura, 20
Lucretia, 113
Lycurgus, 10, 11, 179
Macedon, 78
Manlius, 82
Mantua, 117, 130
Mantuan, 13, 179
Mercury, 39
Milo, 105
Mithridates, 62
Montserrat, 116
Naples, 51
nightingales, 74
nymphs, 115
Octavian Augustus, 76
Oedipus, 110
Olympia, 23
Paris, 130
Penelope, 50
Persians, 80
Petrarch, 139
Philip, 78
Piedmont, 116
Plato, 80

Plutarch, 87
Politian, 125
Polynices, 129
Ptolemy, 101
Quintus Fabius
 Maximus, 96
Rhea, 115
Romans, 30, 43, 82
Rome, 30, 96, 136
Sarah, 42
Sardanapalus, 126
Saturn, 7
satyr, 115
Scipio Africanus, 136
Sempronius
 Gracchus, 96
Siena, 29
Sienese, 30
Solomon, 110
Sophists, 27
Spain, 136
Spartan, 43, 87, 179
spittle house, 111
Taurus, 95
*The Book of the
 Courtier*, 169
Timothy 5:6, 127
Tuscan, 20
urchin, 87
Venetian, 118
Venus, 7
Virginia, 113
wittol, 42

Notes

[1] **Lycurgus** (c. 820 B.C.) was the quasi-legendary legislator of Sparta who implemented the military-oriented reform of Spartan society according to the Oracle of Apollo at Delphi. All his reforms promoted the three Spartan virtues: equality (among citizens), military fitness, and austerity.

[2] *Where dowry comes in freedom comes out* - The man who marries a rich woman loses his autonomy because he will depend on his wife. The recommendation was to marry his peer.

[3] Baptista Spagnuoli Mantuanus (Italian: Battista Mantovano, English: Battista the **Mantuan** or simply **Mantuan**; also known as Johannes Baptista Spagnolo; 17 April 1447 – 22 March 1516) was an Italian Carmelite reformer, humanist, and poet.

Civil Conversation III

⁴ **Juno** was an ancient Roman goddess, the protector and special counselor of the state. She was equated to Hera, queen of the gods in Greek mythology. A daughter of Saturn, she was the wife of Jupiter.

⁵ **Herod** I (c. 72 – 4 or 1 BC), also known as Herod the Great, was a Roman Jewish client king of Judea, referred to as the Herodian kingdom.

⁶ **Hecuba** was a queen in Greek mythology, the wife of King Priam of Troy during the Trojan War.

⁷ **Helen** of Troy, **Helen**, **Helena**, also known as beautiful **Helen**, **Helen** of Argos, or **Helen** of Sparta, was a figure in Greek mythology said to have been the most beautiful woman in the world.

⁸ **Alessio Piemontese**, also known under his Latinized name of **Alexius Pedemontanus**, was the pseudonym of a 16th-century Italian physician, alchemist, and author of the immensely popular book, The **Secrets of Alexis** of Piedmont. His book was published in more than a hundred editions and was still being reprinted in the 1790s. The work was translated into Latin, German, English, Spanish, French, and Polish.

Notes

[9] **Laura**, formerly sometimes known as *Portrait of a Young Bride*, is a painting by the Italian Renaissance master Giorgione. It is the only known painting of the author that was signed and dated by him, it has his name and the date of 1506 on the back. It hangs in the Kunsthistorisches Museum in Vienna, Austria.

[10] **Crates** (c. 365 – c. 285 BC) of Thebes was a Greek Cynic philosopher, the principal pupil of Diogenes of Sinope, and the husband of Hipparchia of Maroneia who lived in the same manner as him. Crates gave away his money to live a life of poverty on the streets of Athens. Respected by the people of Athens, he is remembered for being the teacher of Zeno of Citium, the founder of Stoicism. Various fragments of **Crates'** teachings survive, including his description of the ideal Cynic state.

[11] The **Sophists** held no values other than *winning and succeeding*. They were not true believers in the myths of the Greeks but would use references and quotations from the tales for their own purposes. They were secular atheists, relativists, and cynical about religious beliefs and all traditions.

[12] **James 1:6** KJV (King James Version) – This proverb, *"He who does not do what he must, does not receive what he expects."* has its roots in the

book of James in the bible.

> *But let him ask in faith, nothing wavering. For he that wavereth is like a wave of the sea driven with the wind and tossed. For let not that man think that he shall receive any thing of the Lord. A double minded man is unstable in all his ways.*

[13] **Sarah** (born Sarai) is a biblical matriarch and prophetess, a major figure in Genesis. She was a pious woman, renowned for her hospitality and beauty, the wife and half-sister of Abraham, and the mother of Isaac.

[14] **wittol** - a man who knows of his wife's infidelity and puts up with it.

[15] **Marcus Porcius Cato** "Uticensis" (95 BC – April 46 BC), also known as **Cato** the Younger, was an influential conservative Roman senator during the late Republic.

[16] **Demetrius** I (337–283 BC), also called Poliorcetes was a Macedonian nobleman, military leader, and king of Macedon (294–288 BC). He belonged to the Antigonid dynasty and was its first member to rule Macedonia. He was the son of Antigonus I Monophthalmus and Stratonice.

[17] **Harlot** – a 16th century word for prostitute.

Notes

[18] **The Walnut Tree** is one of **Aesop's fables** and is numbered **250** in the **Perry Index**. It later served as a base for a misogynistic proverb that encourages violence against walnut trees, asses, and women.

[19] **Mithridates** or **Mithradates VI Eupator** (135-63 BC) was the ruler of the Kingdom of Pontus in northern Anatolia from 120 to 63 BC, and one of the Roman Republic's most formidable and determined opponents.

[20] **Hypsicratea** or **Hypsikrateia** (flourished 63 BC), was the concubine, and perhaps wife, of King Mithridates VI of Pontus.

[21] **Homer**, Odyssey (c. 725 BC) - *Few sons, indeed, are like their fathers. Generally they are worse; but just a few are better.* Original Greek: Παῦροι γάρ τοι παῖδες ὁμοῖοι πατρὶ πέλονται, οἱ πλέονες κακίους, παῦροι δέ τε πατρὸς ἀρείους.

[22] **Dante Paradiso Canto VIII, 142-144, 145-148.** Henry Wadsworth Longfellow translation:

> *And if the world below would fix its mind*
> *On the foundation which is laid by nature,*
> *Pursuing that, 'twould have the people good.*
>
> *But you unto religion wrench aside*
> *Him who was born to gird him with the sword,*
> *And make a king of him who is for sermons;*
> *Therefore your footsteps wander from the road.*

23 **Aelius Galenus** or **Claudius Galenus** (September 129 – c. AD 216), often Anglicized as **Galen** or **Galen** of Pergamon, was a Greek physician, surgeon, and philosopher in the Roman Empire. Considered to be one of the most accomplished of all medical researchers of antiquity, **Galen** influenced the development of various scientific disciplines, including anatomy, physiology, pathology, pharmacology, and neurology, as well as philosophy and logic.

24 **Marcus Porcius Cato** (234–149 BC), also known as **Cato the Censor, the Elder,** and **the Wise**, was a Roman soldier, senator, and historian known for his conservatism and opposition to Hellenization. He was the first to write history in Latin with his Origines, a now lost work on the history of Rome.

25 **Caesar Augustus** (23 September 63 BC – 19 August AD 14), also known as **Octavian**, was the first Roman emperor, reigning from 27 BC until his death in AD 14.

26 **Plutarch** (AD 46 – after AD 119) was a Greek Middle Platonist philosopher, historian, biographer, essayist, and priest at the Temple of Apollo in Delphi. He is known primarily for his *Parallel Lives*, a series of biographies of illustrious Greeks and Romans, and *Moralia*, a collection of essays and speeches. *"Return with your shield or on it."* Can be found in **Plutarch's** *Moralia.*

Notes

[27] **Aristippus** of Cyrene (435 – 356 BC) was a hedonistic Greek philosopher and the founder of the Cyrenaic school of philosophy. He was a pupil of Socrates, but adopted a very different philosophical outlook, teaching that the goal of life was to seek pleasure by adapting circumstances to oneself and by maintaining proper control over both adversity and prosperity. His view that pleasure is the only good came to be called ethical hedonism. Despite having two sons, **Aristippus** identified his daughter Arete as the "*intellectual heiress*" of his work.

[28] Lucius Calvenus **Taurus** (286 – 8, second century AD) was a Greek philosopher of the Middle Platonist school.

[29] The **Caspians** were a people of antiquity who dwelt along the southwestern shores of the Caspian Sea, in the region known as Caspiane.

[30] **Ptolemy** I Soter, **Ptolemy** the Savior (367 BC – January 282 BC) was a Macedonian Greek general, historian, and companion of Alexander the Great from the Kingdom of Macedon in northern Greece who became ruler of Egypt, part of Alexander's former empire. On 28 March 284 BC, **Ptolemy** I had **Ptolemy** II, his son, declared king which elevated him to the status of co-regent.

[31] **Charles V** (24 February 1500 – 21 September 1558) was Holy Roman Emperor and Archduke of Austria from 1519 to 1556, King of Spain (Castile and Aragon) from 1516 to 1556, and Lord of the Netherlands as titular Duke of Burgundy from 1506 to 1555. Ultimately, Charles V conceded the Peace of Augsburg and abandoned his multi-national project with a series of abdications in 1556 that divided his hereditary and imperial domains between the Spanish Habsburgs headed by his son Philip II of Spain, and the Austrian Habsburgs headed by his brother Ferdinand, who had been archduke of Austria in Charles's name since 1521 and the designated successor as emperor since 1531.

[32] **Ecclesiasticus 33:19**

> *Good News Bible (GNB):* Never, as long as you live, give anyone power over you — whether son, wife, brother, or friend. Don't give your property to anyone; you might change your mind and have to ask for it back.

> *King James (KG):* Give not thy son and wife, thy brother and friend, power over thee while thou livest, and give not thy goods to another: lest it repent thee, and thou intreat for the same again.

[33] **Milo** of Croton was a 6th-century BC wrestler

from the Magna Graecia city of Croton (in today's Calabria), who enjoyed a brilliant wrestling career and won many victories in the most important athletic festivals of ancient Greece. He was a six-time Olympic victor. He was also said to have carried a bull on his shoulders and to have burst a band about his brow by simply inflating the veins of his temples.

[34] **Aeneas** was a Trojan hero, the son of the Trojan prince Anchises and the Greek goddess Aphrodite. After the Trojan War, as the city burned, **Aeneas** escaped to Latium in Italy, taking his father Anchises and his child Ascanius with him, though his wife Creusa died during the escape.

[35] **Ascanius** (may have reigned between 1176-1138 BC) was a legendary king of Alba Longa and is the son of the Trojan hero Aeneas and Creusa, daughter of Priam.

[36] **David** (flourished c. 1000 BC) was the second king of ancient Israel. He founded the Judaean dynasty and united all the tribes of Israel under a single monarch. His son Solomon expanded the empire that David built.

[37] **Absalom** was the third son of David, King of Israel with Maacah, daughter of Talmai, King of Geshur. 2 Samuel 14:25 describes him as the most

handsome man in the kingdom. Absalom eventually rebelled against his father and was killed during the Battle of Ephraim's Wood.

[38] **Amnon** was, in the Hebrew Bible, the oldest son of King David by his second wife, Ahinoam of Jezreel. He was born in Hebron during his father's reign in Judah. He was the heir apparent to the throne of Israel until he was assassinated by his half-brother Absalom to avenge the rape of Absalom's sister Tamar.

[39] **Oedipus** was a mythical Greek king of Thebes. A tragic hero in Greek mythology, Oedipus accidentally fulfilled a prophecy that he would end up killing his father and marrying his mother, thereby bringing disaster to his city and family.

[40] **Spittle House** was like a hospital. The word spittle is derived from the Middle English word "*spital*" which is the same root as the more modern word "*hospital.*"

[41] *distaff* is a short staff that holds a bundle of fibers of flax or wool ready to be spun into yarn or thread.

[42] **Lucretia** (died c. 510 BC), anglicized as Lucrece, was a noblewoman in ancient Rome whose rape by Sextus Tarquinius (Tarquin) and subsequent suicide precipitated a rebellion that overthrew the Roman monarchy and led to the

transition of the Roman government from a kingdom to a republic.

[43] **Virginia** (about 450 BC) was a beautiful plebian girl and the daughter of Lucius Verginius, a respected centurion.

[44] **Rhea** (or Rea) Silvia, also known as Ilia (as well as other names) was the mythical mother of the twins Romulus and Remus, who founded the city of Rome.

[45] Giovanni **Boccaccio** (1313 in Certaldo in Tuscany – December 21, 1375) is a Florentine writer. His work in Tuscan, notably his collection of short stories the Decameron, which had enormous success, makes him considered one of the creators of Italian prose literature.

[46] Agnolo (Angelo) Ambrogini (14 July 1454 – 24 September 1494), commonly known by his nickname Poliziano; anglicized as **Politian**; was an Italian classical scholar and poet of the Florentine Renaissance.

[47] **Sardanapalus**, supposed to have lived in the 7th century BC, is portrayed as a decadent figure who, spends his life in self-indulgence and dies in an orgy of destruction.

[48] **Timothy 5:6**

> *KJV (King James):* But she that liveth in pleasure is dead while she liveth.

BBE (Basic Bible in English): But she who gives herself to pleasure is dead while she is living.

⁴⁹ The Book of **Judith** is a deuterocanonical book. It tells of a Jewish widow, **Judith**, who uses her beauty and charm to destroy an Assyrian general and save Israel from oppression.

⁵⁰ In the deuterocanonical Book of Judith, **Holofernes** was an invading Assyrian general known for having been beheaded by Judith, a Hebrew widow who entered his camp and beheaded him while he was drunk.

⁵¹ **Eteocles** and **Polynices** were the sons of the classic Greek tragic hero and Theban king Oedipus, who fought each other for the control of Thebes after their father abdicated, ultimately killing each other in a battle for control of the city.

⁵² The **Battle of Saint-Quentin** of 1557 was a decisive engagement, during the Italian War of 1551-1559, between the Kingdom of France and the Habsburg Empire, at Saint-Quentin in Picardy. A Habsburg Spanish force under Duke Emmanuel Philibert of Savoy defeated a French army under the command of Duke Louis Gonzaga and Duke Anne de Montmorency.

Notes

[53] Publius Cornelius **Scipio Africanus** (236/235–183 BC) was a Roman general and statesman, most notable as one of the main architects of Rome's victory against Carthage in the Second Punic War. Often regarded as one of the best military commanders and strategists of all time, his greatest military achievement was the defeat of Hannibal at the Battle of Zama in 202 BC. This victory in Africa earned him the epithet Africanus, literally meaning "the African," but meant to be understood as a conqueror of Africa.

[54] **Hannibal** (247 – between 183 and 181 BC) was a Carthaginian general and statesman who commanded the forces of Carthage in their battle against the Roman Republic during the Second Punic War. He is widely regarded as one of the greatest military commanders in history.

[55] Lucius Cornelius Scipio **Asiaticus** (3rd century BC – after 183 BC) was a general and statesman of the Roman Republic. He was the son of Publius Cornelius Scipio and the younger brother of Scipio Africanus. He was elected consul in 190 BC, and later that year led (with his brother) the Roman forces to victory at the Battle of Magnesia, West Central Asia.

[56] The **Gordian Knot** is an Ancient Greek legend of Phrygian Gordium associated with Alexander the Great who is said to have cut the knot in 333

BC. It is often used as a metaphor for an intractable problem (untying an impossibly tangled knot) solved easily by finding an approach to the problem that renders the perceived constraints of the problem moot ("cutting the **Gordian knot**").

[57] **Francesco Petrarch** (20 July 1304 – 18/19 July 1374) – from Sonnet 53,

> ...
> *When behold thy ministers (I' know not whence:)*
> *To give me to part, who to his destiny*
> *Woe to him who contrasts, woe to him who hides.*

[58] **Homer** was the author of the Iliad and the Odyssey, the two epic poems that are the foundational works of ancient Greek literature.

[59] **Achilles** was a hero of the Trojan War in Greek mythology, the greatest of all the Greek warriors, and the central character of Homer's Iliad. He was the son of the Nereid Thetis and Peleus, king of Phthia.

[60] **Sexton** is a church officer or employee who takes care of the church property and performs related minor duties (such as ringing the bell for services and digging graves).

Notes

[61] A **galley** is a type of ship propelled by rowers that originated in the eastern Mediterranean Sea and was used for warfare, trade, and piracy from the first millennium BC.

[62] *"As many servants so many enemies."* was a quote by Lucius Annaeus Seneca the Younger (c. 4 BC – 65 AD), usually known by the mononym Seneca, was a Stoic philosopher of Ancient Rome, a statesman, dramatist, and, in one word, satirist, from the post-Augustan age of Latin literature.

[63] The saying *"The eye of the master fattens the horse,"* can also be said in a more understanding phrase, *"It's the master's eye that makes the mill go."*

[64] **The Book of the Courtier** by Baldassare Castiglione is a lengthy philosophical dialogue on the topic of what constitutes an ideal courtier or (in the third chapter) court lady, worthy to befriend and advise a Prince or political leader. Inspired by the Spanish court during his time as Ambassador of the Holy See (1524–1529), Castiglione set the narrative of the book in his years as a courtier in his native Duchy of Urbino.

Made in the USA
Middletown, DE
05 August 2023